DARE
TO SEE
differently

DARE
TO SEE
differently

**Re-Imaging Reality
from a Feminist Point of View**

John D'Mello

**auline
PUBLICATIONS**

Cover design: Bro. Melroy Fernandes

Cover: Nilesh Bhagwe

ISBN 81-7176-500-9

www.paulineindia.org

*Pauline Publications is an activity of the Daughters of St Paul,
an international religious congregation, using the communications
media to spread the gospel message and to promote the dignity
of all people.*

Printed by Tresa Nirappel at St Paul Press Training School, Bandra,
Mumbai. Published by the Pauline Sisters Bombay Society, 143
Waterfield Road, Bandra, Mumbai 400 050. Tel: 26424081,
26436188, Fax: (022) 26518543 e-mail: editorial@paulineindia.org
2006

Contents

Preface

ॐ

As ecclesiastical advisor to the Catholic Women's Council, India, on social and theological matters for the last 6 years, I always questioned my role and presence in the group. I often asked *'what am I, a male, doing here in this Council of women?'* The answer I generally received from the women was: *"Your presence is important! By including a male viewpoint we arrive at a more comprehensive perspective!"*

What edified me is that these women were interested in a more complete, more holistic perspective. The word 'feminist' for them, did not just mean "inclusive of women's experiences" but it meant something far more. It meant "respectful of both sexes". It meant a more "egalitarian" perspective. This is also the standpoint of this booklet.

All the knowledge we receive is filtered through a lens. This lens is the traditional, one-sided, androcentric, 'male' way of thinking. This image of the world cannot be allowed to remain unaltered. **We need to "see" differently.** We need to shatter old lenses and transmit a new viewpoint, which combines the perspective of both sexes. When women include their own experiences in their telling of reality, they are altering or modifying the traditional 'male' view of the world, they are re-imaging and presenting a more complete picture of reality. Similarly, when men include a feminist perspective in their description of the world, they are likewise re-imaging and transmitting this new all-inclusive point of view. Such re-imaging is essential to develop a more egalitarian, comprehensive, and androgenous perspective. Only if we shatter traditional lenses, **only if we dare to see differently,** can we make any headway towards a genuine equity of relations in Church and Society

This booklet comprises a series of reflections, which initially appeared in the Neythri columns, over a period of four years (1997 — 2000). They can be arranged in four sections:

The **first section** consists of sample instances of biblical re-readings: six of them from the New Testament and six of them from the Old Testament. In the **second section** the feminist perspective 'confronts' some burning contemporary issues and problems. Approximately 14 issues are chosen. The **third section** recounts "her stories": six stories of exceptional women, who showed by their lives, how the world could be more equitably transformed: Mother Teresa, Pandita Ramabai, Aung San Suu Kyi, Diana Ortiz, Tasleema Nasreen and Medha Patkar. This selection of women does not pretend to be comprehensive. Several other exceptional women no doubt could also have been chosen, but the criterion was to present and discuss thematic qualities, relevant to women's issues.

The entire purpose of this compilation is to stimulate the process of "Feminization of the Church" (read, render an environment of equal relations within the Church). Accordingly, the last section concludes with three articles, one summarizing the various paradigms for such feminization, another drawing on images of the early Christian model of women's empowerment, and a third describing actual experiments to implement the process. The underlying hope (as declared in the book *Bread and Roses*) is that "the rising of women implies the rising of the entire human race".

John D'Mello
Professor, Mumbai Seminary, June 2002
Ecclesiastical Advisor to the CCWI (Catholic Women's Council of India),

Foreword

℘

For several years, from 1989-1998, I was Chairperson of the Laity Commission of the Catholic Bishops' Conference of India. The Women's Desk was attached to this Commission in 1992. It became a full-fledged Commission in 1996. It was during these years that I had occasions to get more acquainted with the sufferings of women all over the world and especially in our country. It was an education to learn first-hand of the ground realities endured by women.

Some of these realities have been outlined in the final statement of the recent Asian Meeting on Women, organized by the Federation of Asian Bishops' Conference ("Women's God-Experiences Rooted in Life", Bishops' Institute of Lay Apostolate (BILA III) at Thailand, October 15-21, 2001):

- *"Within the overall context of poverty and deprivation, the situation of women is most dehumanizing. This is aggravated by economic globalization.*

- *Violence against women such as rape, wife battering, molestation, incest, and trafficking of women are common to all the countries.*

- *Female foeticide and infanticide, dowry deaths, and discriminatory practices against female children as well as against widows, divorced and abandoned women are widespread in some parts of Asia.*

- *In almost all the countries women are discriminated against because of their gender. Sadly, this is often legitimized by religio-cultural practices."*

Women constitute half of humankind. By discriminating against them and suppressing their capabilities we are doing a disservice to society and hindering its progress. We have to remind ourselves, also, that women as mothers shape the future of society, so well expressed in the saying, "the hand that rocks the cradle rules the world". By restricting the growth of women, we stunt the growth of whole generations. What is even worse, when we discriminate against women, we are doing injustice to people we love dearly—our mothers, wives, sisters, daughters, friends and the army of religious women who render outstanding service to our church.

This book by John D'Mello, Professor of Philosophy and Sociology, at St Pius College, Goregaon (the Archdiocesan Seminary of Mumbai), is a collection of articles, which initially appeared in the **Neythri**, the bulletin of the Catholic Women's Council of India. Before I read them in the manuscript of this book I had already read them in the original. As soon as I received the **Neythri**, I would first have a look at John D'Mello's columns. They were always original and thought-provoking. I am glad that he has brought them together in this publication because they can now be available to a wider reading public.

This book must be read with discernment, reflectively and assessed by the reader against the background of his/her own experience. It is a book that could help to form one's own convictions in the matter so that these can lead to attitudes, actions and decisions that, on a day-to-day basis, would favour the cause of women. John D'Mello comes across, in the book, as an ardent defender of women's issues. One can see that he feels, deeply, the various sufferings women undergo and he speaks passionately from their point of view. This is an excellent example for men in general because women's issues are not the preserve of women alone. In fact, they would benefit greatly from the support of men who understand what women are going through.

I hope that this book will help us to understand a little better the capabilities of women, and inspire us to reflect on the feminine genius and on the fruits of feminine holiness that have been referred to by Holy Father, Pope John Paul II in his Apostolic Letter "Mulieris Dignitatem":

> "Therefore the Church gives thanks for each and every woman: for mothers, for sisters, for wives, for women consecrated to God in virginity; . . . for women who watch over the human persons in the family; for women who work professionally, and are at times burdened with a great social responsibility . . . the church gives thanks for all the manifestations of the feminine "genius" which have appeared in the course of history, in the midst of all peoples and nations, she gives thanks for all the charisms, which the Holy Spirit distributes to women in the history of the People of God, for all the victories which she owes to their faith, hope and charity; she gives thanks for all the fruits of feminine holiness. . . . Meditating on the biblical mystery of the "woman", the Church prays that in this mystery all women may discover themselves and their "supreme vocation" (No.31).

+ Bosco Penha
Auxiliary Bishop
Archdiocese of Bombay

I A

Feminist Biblical Re-readings:

New Testament

I A

Feminist Biblical Re-readings: New Testament

1
Feminist Theology
*"The Unnamed Woman
Who will Always be Remembered. . ."*
ᘓ

One of the greatest revolutions of the twentieth century was neither the revolution in sex, nor the revolution in communist countries, nor the revolution in technology, but surprisingly, the revolution in knowledge. We have come to realize today that all knowledge is *perspectival*. Put simply, it means that all knowledge comes from a particular viewpoint. This has tremendous consequences.

Earlier, for instance, we referred to the year 1857 as the year of the "Sepoy Mutiny". Nowadays, history books refer to the event as the "First Indian Uprising for Independence". This is not just a change of words, but a complete change of perspective. History books written by the British saw the 1857 war as a mutiny, whereas Indian history books see the same event as a struggle for independence. Thus, an entire history can be rewritten and reinterpreted depending on the perspective of the writer.

It is the same with theology and with the interpretation of scripture. Until the last few decades theology was written mainly from a male perspective. Most books on theology and on Scripture were written in First World countries and predominantly by males. As a result, the experiences of women, especially the experiences of Third World women were largely ignored. When scriptural interpretation was given, insights which brought out a woman's perspective were either forgotten or overlooked. Likewise, when Church History was being studied, since it was men who were doing the study, the stories of women, the roles of women, and their functions in the early church were unconsciously disregarded.

Women theologians today would like to recapture some of the biblical insights, which may have been simply neglected or omitted. Feminist theologians would like to focus on roles that women played in the early church and give a more complete picture of Church History. They call this "restoring history back to women".[1] All this requires a paradigm shift in theology. From a male-centred or androcentric world view, the shift has to be towards an androgenous or 'mutually respectful' world view.

Lest all this remains up in the air, this shift of perspective can be illustrated with a concrete example. Take the story of the unnamed woman with the alabaster box of ointment, which is mentioned in all the four gospels (Mk 14:3-9; Mt 26:6-13; Lk 7:36-50 and Jn 12:1-8). The original version is that of Mark and is paralleled by Matthew. Luke and John have made adaptations to suit their own didactic purposes.

This unnamed woman has been wrongly slandered, referred to as Mary Magdalene, called a prostitute, labelled a 'waster of perfume'. In fact, she was none of these things.[2] Traditionally, the emphasis in the story is on forgiveness (the woman sinned much, loved much and so, much was *forgiven*). There are many aspects of the story however, which have escaped attention.

1. What has not been noticed generally is the *boldness and the courage* of the woman who gate-crashed into a house full of men. In a society where women were considered 'inferior in status', where women were not allowed to learn the *Talmud*, the courage to enter a company of select men was indeed an act of intrepidity and daring.

2. She was *the first woman* to *acknowledge Jesus as the Messiah*. This is the significance of her symbolic gesture of anointing. Only Messiahs were anointed. Alabaster or oil was a precious commodity to a desert people in a dry land and so they spoke metaphorically of receiving God's spirit as "being anointed".

3. Not only did she acknowledge Jesus as the Messiah, but also, while Peter and the other disciples misunderstood the nature of that messianic role (imagining it to be glorious and triumphant), *she alone grasped its true nature*. She alone understood that the Messiah had to challenge the powers that be and so suffer and die. Her anointing was an anointing for burial.

4. It is for this reason that the evangelist put into the mouth of Jesus one of the greatest compliments to any disciple *"Your name will always be remembered, wherever the gospel is preached"*.

This interpretation brings out the prophetic character of women. It is very different from the story of a woman who loved much, who cried much, who was a notorious sinner, and who dabbled in perfume. Such an interpretation can be a source of inspiration and courage to other women who may have the opportunity to challenge corrupt powers and attempt daring symbolic actions.

This is an instance of feminist hermeneutics (interpretation of scripture) and this is what feminist theology is all about. Feminist theology is one stream of liberation theology. It is called a liberation theology because it seeks to emancipate theology from its male-centredness and make it truly respectful of both sexes. No wonder feminist theologians today are the most prolific of writers, producing a very large number of books on theology!!

17

2
Re-imaging Mary

I n my history of preparing couples for marriage, one comment I have heard expressed quite often is that 'the bride is very beautiful' while 'the bridegroom in comparison seems quite ordinary!' and vice-versa. 'The man is quite handsome' while 'the woman seems plain and ordinary!' The common explanations given for these 'apparent' mismatches are that love is blind; beauty lies in the eye of the beholder; love goes beyond exterior looks and so on. But these explanations, to me, are only part of the answer.

The real answer, it seems to me, is that we never really love *just* the person. What we love also is the *image* of the person we have in our minds. Here is a person, for instance, whom I think is wonderful and I ask with genuine surprise: 'How is it that other people don't love this person as I do, being such a wonderful person that he or she is? The answer is that he or she is a wonderful person no doubt, but it does not appear so to others. I have idealized him or her in my mind and I love and worship that extraordinary image, which to others does not appear so extraordinary after all. So it is the image, which is the medium through which my love for a person becomes real.

Now this should not be shocking. It does not mean that I have to go around telling people that I don't love you, but I love the image that I have of you. But it does mean that that the image we have of people is **crucial**.

18

It is an aid to action. If we need to raise the level of the way we treat those around us, *we need to raise the level of our image of them.* If I have a low image of someone I tend to disrespect that person or, at the very most, I may have pity, but I can never really love that person. But if on the contrary, I have a high image of that person, I will love and admire that person.

What about most images, pictures and icons of Mary? There is a danger that she can be depicted quite often as a woman with head bowed, with shoulders hunched, a pained, sorrowful expression on her face, depicting an attitude of passivity and resignation, and written across the picture the caption: "Thy Will be Done". In other words, the image of Mary that comes across is one of submissiveness, acquiescence, and passive compliance. Even the titles we give to Mary would reflect this—Mother of Sorrows, Mother of Dolours, Mother most Obedient, Mother most Meek, Mother most Mild. This is not an image that can inspire young women of today, who are seeking to be dynamic, vibrant, enthusiastic, assertive and independent.

If Mary is the model for all Christian mothers, if Mary is the type for every Christian woman, then the qualities that such images or icons would tend to inspire are: passivity, obedience, resignation and compliance, all of which support a subordinate role for women.[3]

It is for this reason that Feminist Scripture Scholars have plunged into the study of scriptures, focusing on those aspects that have been missed out by other scholars and have drawn up entirely different images of Mary. Here are a few of them.

Mary, an Initiator: At the wedding feast of Cana in Galilee, Mary is the one who notices the shortage of wine and appeals to Jesus. Jesus begins to give an excuse, but Mary pays no attention and tells the servants to do his bidding. So Mary becomes the one who initiates the *first sign* of the 'reign of God'.

Mary, a Woman of Courage: The 'Yes' said by Mary at the Annunciation required tremendous courage. To accept a child outside of the conjugal union, she had to go against the rigid Jewish tradition, against her family, against her village, against her husband-to-be and against the high priests. It was an act of great independence and assertiveness. Again, during the Passion, when all the other apostles scuttled and disappeared underground, Mary remained faithful and loyal, courageously accompanying Jesus all the way and standing by the Cross till the very end.[4]

Mary, a Leader: Even after the death of Jesus, when the apostles were still scared and fearful, Mary was probably the rallying point for the group. Acts 1:14 suggests that Mary and the apostles met frequently as a group in private homes, and it is probably at one of these homes (with Mary being present) that Pentecost took place and where the apostles convened, planned, organized themselves and from where they went forth to preach the good news.

It is true that much of the violence inflicted on women (rape, wife battering, dowry harassment, female foeticide, eve teasing, sexual harassment and exploitation) is because of the low status and low image of women in society. This is the only explanation for the high rate of illiteracy of women compared to men (46 % compared to 25 %) and the low ratio of women to men in our population (933 compared to 1000).[5] Given these facts, it is time that we in the Catholic Church, begin by updating our own image of Mary, the model and type for all Christian women. It is only then that we will raise the level of our image of all women.

3
Was St Paul a Woman-hater?
ℭ

In this age of feminist consciousness, one of the questions that is asked very often is this: was St Paul a woman-hater or a male chauvinist? There are at least two instances in his epistles where he prescribes prohibitions for women that seem to be discriminatory.

1. Women should not pray in public without covering their heads. (I Cor 11:5)

2. Women should not speak in church meetings. If they want to find out about something they should ask their husbands at home. (I Cor 14:34-36)

I think the question has to be looked at in the context of both the words and actions of Paul. Paul is the one who encouraged women to be church leaders, to be his co-workers and to pray and prophesy as the examples of Priscilla, Phoebe, Nympha, Claudia, Lydia and the four daughters of Philip of Caesarea illustrate. Paul was a great believer of equality and mutual respect. His words became the famous baptismal formula: "And now there are no more distinctions among you, between Jew and Greek, between slave and free person, *between male and female.* You are all one in Christ Jesus!" (Gal 3:28). If Paul believed in equality, how then does one explain the above two instances.

In the first instance, Paul is referring solely to Corinthian women. In those days at the centre of the city of Corinth stood the temple of Aphrodite with a thousand priestess-prostitutes attached to it. The city was rife with all manner of sects, religious cults and mystery religions, which taught self-gratification and sexual exploits as ways to spiritual liberation. In Corinth it was only the temple prostitutes who shaved their heads as a mark of devotion to the goddess of fertility and it was the women of the spirit cults who let their unbound hair fall all around them as they sang and danced around the altar.

Paul wanted Christian women to be distinct from these women and Christian liturgy not to be confused with the rites of the mystery cults. Hence, he prescribed that Christian women, when taking part in public worship, or when prophesying or proclaiming God's message, should not shave their heads and should not leave their hair unbound, but should have it covered. Concernedly, Paul believed he was only trying to safeguard order and decorum in the liturgy, while prescribing liturgical rules for women.[6]

The second instance, according to many Scripture scholars, is not Pauline in origin. It is quite possibly an interpolation by a later editor. Verses 34-36 appear out of place and interrupt the smooth flow of thought from 33 to 37. More importantly, it contradicts Paul's general focus on equality. The anonymous editor is only reflecting the traditional code of hierarchical relationships, whereby married women, prevented from studying the Torah, were expected to clarify their questions at home, rather than hold up public meetings.[7]

New Testament authors in general were very much influenced by the culture of their times. They lived in a patriarchal society where 'man' was accepted as the head of the household and 'men' exercised most of the leadership in public life at that time. By and large, Paul too accepts this basic social structure. Nevertheless, it is interesting that, in contrast to the general culture, Paul still makes mention of equality. Even more, at times he comes across as trying to mitigate or blunt a situation of inequality whenever he could.

Thus, when he says that 'woman came from man,' he follows it up with 'just as man comes through woman.' And when he asked women to submit to their husbands, (according to the traditional pattern of relationships), he immediately added the injunction that husbands should love and 'serve' their wives, insisting thereby that the relationship, between husband and wife should always be based on love and respect. For Paul, the guiding principle was that woman is not independent of man nor man independent of woman.

In short, Paul can hardly be called a woman-hater or male chauvinist. Instead, we might rather say that Jewish society at the time was patriarchal and Paul, though largely a product of his culture, shows faint traces of breaking through that cultural mould.

4
Jesus and the Canaanite Woman
Going Beyond our Narrow Circles
※

Christians in India tend to suffer from a minority complex. When there is an injustice done to our community or to members of our community, we get incensed. Yet when atrocities are being perpetrated on others, we seldom get roused enough to take action.

In 1990 two nuns were murdered in a slum in Jogeshwari, Mumbai. The next day their characters were assassinated by a false report in the national dailies. The press did not apologize for the blunder. The police were not able to find the culprits. A year later there was a rally held to protest against the inactivity of the police and the irresponsibility of the press. Participating in this rally were 71 different women's organizations, the vast majority of whom were secular and non-Christian. It was a sterling example of sisterhood. For these secular organizations, the issue of violence against women was primary. They had no hesitation in moving beyond the narrow circles of religion and joining in solidarity. These women's organizations set a shining example.

In the early Church too, one of the major problems of the Christian Jews was whether or not to go beyond their circle and include Gentiles at their table fellowship. The gospels of Mark (7:24-30) and Matthew (15:20-28) frame a response through the story of the Syro-Phoenician or Canaanite woman.

24

This Gentile woman had asked Jesus to cure her daughter. Jesus' first answer is that he has to cater to the house of Israel. Teasingly, he says, "It is not fair to take food from the children and throw it to the house dogs." But the woman retorts, "Yes, but even the house dogs eat the scraps that fall from the children's table!" thus getting the better of Jesus in a battle of wits.

What is even more unique about the story is the fact that the Gentile woman apparently obliges Jesus to re-think his mission or at least to see the situation in a different way. She seems to have enabled him to act in a way apparently blocked to him before.[8] The story is meant to respond to the conflict within the early church over the issue of including Gentiles.

The Gentile woman's story can stimulate us as well. Often, Christian groups tend to join hands with other women's groups only when their own interest is affected. Following from the gospel story, it is imperative for every woman's organization to join hands with sister groups on common issues. At a second level, every woman's organization needs to network at the international level with similar organizations in other countries. And lastly, it has become more and more crucial for women's organizations to collaborate with other oppressed groups, like workers, Dalits and tribals. The struggles of women are linked to the struggles of these other groups. Only in this way can a united front be formed. Otherwise the insight from the Gentile woman's intervention in the gospel will have gone in vain. . . .

5
The Story of Martha and Mary
(Lk 10:38-42)
A Feminist Interpretation
☙

I once attended a parish council meeting and the meeting had hardly begun when the parish priest asked one of the women present to go into the kitchen and prepare tea for the council members. The woman looked surprised. Later, she confided to me: "There were so many men present, yet only I, *a woman*, was asked to go inside and prepare tea! Are we women meant only to look after bodily refreshment?" she asked, half-jokingly.

Perhaps her comment was justified, in view of the usual interpretation given of the story of Martha and Mary. In former times, whenever I heard this passage being read, I was always a bit upset. Martha was the one who was doing all the work and yet she is the one who gets scolded by Jesus. It seemed very unfair. The interpretation traditionally given was that Martha's role represented *work*, and Mary's role (the better part) represented *prayer*. So, prayer was better than work or contemplation was better than action.

Later, I found that this particular interpretation was the result of specific historical preoccupations,[9] emphasized in the context of a debate among religious orders. One group, the radical group, kept insisting that the role of religious orders was to go out of the monasteries and get involved in social work, schools,

26

hospitals, etc The other group, the traditional group, believed that the role of religious was to remain within the precincts of the cloister and pray, contemplate. The answer given to settle this debate was that contemplation (Mary's part) was superior to action (Martha's part). But this of course was in the Middle Ages.

Today, several Biblical historians have made a study of the household churches of the early Christian communities and find that there existed a conflict of functions in these churches—the ministry of service (represented by Martha) as opposed to the Ministry of the Word (represented by Mary).[10] The Lukan story reflects this conflict and admits of two interpretations.

One interpretation sees Luke as criticizing the '*attitude* of being overly concerned about activity' (represented by Martha) and favouring the *attitude* of listening to the word (represented by Mary).[11] If these refer to the role of women in the early churches, then discipleship for women means an attitude of listening rather than an attitude oriented to activity. This interpretation downplays the role of women, which, though in keeping with the rest of Luke's work (especially Acts of the Apostles) is unlike Paul's. The Pauline epistles constantly mention stories of women who were very active in the early church— women preachers, women missionaries, prophets and founders of house-churches.

A second interpretation sees Luke as subordinating the ministry of table service (Martha's role) to the Ministry of the Word (Mary's role). There was a conservative opinion in the early church, which wished to restrict woman's function to the merely practical one of table service (which probably included preparation of a meal, purchase and distribution of food, actual serving during the meal, and possibly cleaning up afterwards).[12] According to this second interpretation, Luke disapproves of this conservative opinion and instead commends

Mary's abandonment of this traditional domestic role and favours her assuming the position of a disciple. Discipleship for women according to this interpretation means participating in the Ministry of the Word. Mary's "choosing the better part" is seen as a great stride for theological education of women, especially at a time when studying of the Torah was prohibited for women.[13]

Whatever be the interpretation we choose to follow, it is evident that woman's role in education of the faith is vital. It is not that women have better pedagogical methods, but rather the values that a child picks up at its mother's knees, are the values that it will cherish for the rest of its life. It is said *"Educate a man and you educate just one person; educate a woman and you educate an entire family!"* This statement is very true of the Indian situation. And since the Church is like a family, the education of the people of God will never be quite complete if women are not allowed to take an active part in explaining and interpreting the word of God.

6
Who was Mary Magdalene?

Repentant 'Prostitute' or 'Apostle to the Apostles'?

＊＊＊ cʃ ＊＊＊

One of the great confusions in the history of the Church (a confusion which has been detrimental to the image of women in general) has been the unwarranted identification of Mary Magdalene with the image of a prostitute or sinner. In fact, this identification became pronounced in the Western Church only from the sixth century. In the Eastern Church, Mary Magdalene was always treated as separate from Mary of Bethany and distinct from the unnamed sinner. Who really then was Mary Magdalene?

First of all, we must begin by stating who Mary Magdalene was not. She was:

* NOT a prostitute
* NOT the unnamed sinner who anointed Jesus and wiped his feet with her hair (this may have been some other person, but not Mary Magdalene)
* NOT Mary of Bethany, the sister of Martha and Lazarus (this Mary, who anointed Jesus, was from Bethany, while Mary Magdalene came 'from Magdala')
* NOT the adulteress who was about to be stoned in John's gospel

Who then was Mary Magdalene? She was:

1. *A woman who was grateful to Jesus because he had cured her of her sickness.* Lk 8:1-3 refers to Mary of Magdalene as 'one from whom seven demons had been expelled'. This is a Jewish expression for 'one who was sick or possessed'.

2. *A follower of Jesus*: She is always mentioned among the women who followed Jesus and travelled with him through the towns and villages. In fact, after Peter, James, John and Judas, her name figures as the most frequently mentioned follower of Jesus—14 times in all.

3. *A woman of great courage*: She remained with Jesus right unto the very end, till Calvary, unlike the apostles who ran away.

4. *The First Witness of the Resurrection*: She was one of the myrrh-bearing women who went early in the morning to the tomb to anoint Jesus and was privileged to be the first to see him after the Resurrection. Jesus gave her the commission to pass on the news to the apostles. For this reason, she has been called 'Apostle to the Apostles'.

Why then did the mix-up take place? It was Gregory the Great (540—604 CE) who, in his homily on Repentance and Forgiveness [homily 33] and very much influenced by the penitential theology of that time, identified Mary Magdalene with the sinner of Lk 7:36-50.[14] And when the seven demons were understood as the seven capital sins, the mistake was compounded further. From then on (in the Western Church) Mary Magdalene was the sinner/prostitute turned saint. This mythic image of a sainted "sinner" even led to a pornographic movement in 19th century England, where poor women were manipulated into posing for 'Magdalene photos'. In many places throughout Europe 'Magdalene Houses' were established to care for women who had experienced an abused life of prostitution.[15] Until 1969, her feast day

30

was entitled "St Mary Magdalene, Penitent", the gospel reading was from Luke 7:36-50 and the Roman Breviary referred to her as 'The Great Sinner'. From a woman's point of view, we might say that it was natural for a male clergy to stereotype or cast her into the role of 'Eve': sinner, weak woman, given to the flesh, temptress, prostitute, so as to more strongly contrast it with her conversion patterned on the new 'Eve': pure, holy, chaste, forgiven much, because she loved much. Thus Mary Magdalene's personality was split into two: her life before conversion and her life after conversion. Among the eastern churches, on the other hand, no such confusion took place. She was always given the titles of "Myrrh-Bearer", "Equal to the Apostles" and spoken of as "Primary Witness" of the Paschal Mystery of Christ.

It was only in 1969 with the Reform of the Liturgical calendar in the Western Church and critical reading of the NT that all references to her being a "sinner" and "penitent" were removed and her feast day, July 22, was titled simply: Mary Magdalene, Memorial. Unfortunately however her status in the Roman calendar still ranks as a memorial and is not yet elevated to a feast. This prompted Ruth Fox to remark: *"Even though Mary Magdalene has been recognized through the centuries as 'apostle to the apostles' (see John Paul II, "On the Dignity and Vocation of Women," # 16), she ranks below the Twelve in the Liturgy."*[16]

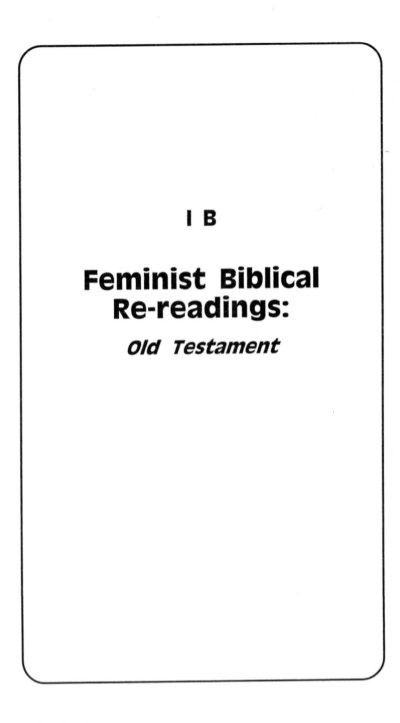

I B

Feminist Biblical Re-readings:

Old Testament

7
The Story of Dinah
Victims of Rape
↭

On August 24, 1997, the Indian Express reported the shocking incident of the rape of a **106-year-old widow** by a 50-year-old man in the South-West section of Delhi. It was significant that the widow could neither speak, nor hear nor see clearly.

7 months earlier, there was another horrifying piece of news in the Asian Age, January 20, 1997, viz., that a **3-year-old girl** was raped by a man at Dharavi, Sion, Mumbai.

These incidents remind me very much of the famous case of Mathura in 1979, which catalyzed the women's movement. Mathura was a 16-year-old tribal girl from Maharashtra, who was raped by two policemen in the police compound. The Supreme Court in reversing the judgement of the Bombay high court and acquitting the two policemen, gave the argument that Mathura *had not "actively resisted intercourse with the two men"*. [How could she when her aggressors were in a position of power?]. Much later, as a result of nation-wide consciousness aroused by this case, an amendment was made to the law viz., that in a custodial situation, *'passive submission under threat'* by a woman cannot be considered 'consent'.[17]

In the Bible too there are at least two stories of rape and in both instances the same 'helpless' situation of women is apparent.

1. In chapter 34 of Genesis, *Dinah*, the daughter of Jacob and Leah, was raped by Shechem, a Hivite. Thereafter, Shechem agreed to marry Dinah and the arrangement was accepted by her brothers, Simeon and Levi, on the condition that Shechem and the whole clan of Hivites circumcised themselves and became Jews. They consented. On the third night, when the pain of circumcision is the greatest, Simeon and Levi crept up on the Hivites and cruelly massacred all of them. They avenged the abomination of their sister, but in the process completed the circle of violence. Throughout the whole episode, Dinah's wishes are of no account. She is not allowed to have a choice or will or mind of her own. Decisions are just taken for her and she has absolutely no say in the matter.

2. The second instance is narrated in chapter 19 of the book of Judges. It is truly a sad story. A *Levite and his mistress*, travelling to Jerusalem find hospitality with an old man at Gibeah. A gang of Benjaminites knock on the door and want the Levite to come out and allow himself to be sodomized. Instead, the Levite offers his mistress to the rowdy Benjaminites, who then proceed to gang rape the concubine the entire night, eventually leading to her death. The poor concubine is a pawn in the entire episode. Her attitude is one of 'helpless surrender'. She is just "offered" as a sacrifice on the altar of the men's animal desires. She has no voice.

What is common in all instances of rape is the vulnerability of women, the helplessness of the victims, their passive and defenseless submission, and their inability to cry out, resist and seek justice. What is equally clear is that in all instances the men concerned are in positions of superiority and power.

This unequal structure of power is called 'patriarchy' and so long as our culture enforces, permits and maintains this unequal situation, there will always be possibilities of violence against women. This is the root cause of all the sexual harassment in offices (where the boss is usually a man, who controls the salary), of marital rape (where the husband is the dominant partner), of custodial rape (where policemen, wardens or public servants abuse their office) as well as of any other type of rape (where the woman is defenseless).

Our culture exhibits numerous expressions of patriarchy. Some of them are clearly discriminatory, for instance, an unequal wage structure, unequal educational opportunities, women being confined to house and kitchen work, dowry or payment for the upkeep of a woman, marriage/divorce laws biased in favour of men and advertisements that exploit women as sex-objects. Others are more symbolic, like the father "giving away" his daughter in marriage, a bride taking on her husband's surname, and marriage ceremonies that include the 'obey' clause for women. Unfortunately, at times agencies that should normally fight against these patriarchal structures, *reinforce them*, like the judiciary and the Church. It has been reported that while cases of rape all over India are on the increase, convictions of rapists are on the decrease.[18] Naturally, because most judges are men. In the Church too there are patriarchal structures and quite often this is evident in its teachings, in its theology and in its interpretation of Scriptures.

So long then, as women continue to be in unequal relationships with men, there will always be the possibility of violence against women. And so long as this situation of patriarchy persists in Indian society, women will continue to be raped every 54 minutes. That is why Susan Griffin, in *Rape: the Politics of Consciousness*, understands rape as "the crime of annihilation of the woman as a human being."[19] Therefore to struggle against patriarchy and the structures associated with it is not only to be feminist but to be truly Christian.

8
Queen Vashti
Sexual Stereotypes
❧

A stereotype is a notion, which conforms to an *unjustifiably* fixed or standardized mental picture. Sexual stereotypes are those which assume *unjustifiable* differences between males and females. Florence Howe recalls how, as a young girl, when she and her brother were being introduced at family gatherings, she would hear comments like "Isn't it a pity that *she has all the brains* and *he has all the looks*?" This is a typical example of a *sexual stereotype*, where it is assumed that men are supposed to be smart and women are supposed to be dumb but beautiful.

Sexual stereotypes, she says, start early. "We learn about sex roles very early in our lives probably within the first few months of birth." We learn these roles through relatively simple patterns that most of us take for granted. We place girl-babies in pink cribs and dress them in pink, lemon yellow or light blue; while boy babies are dressed in navy blue or brown. "We throw boy-babies up in the air and play rough games with them. We coo over girl-babies and handle them delicately. We encourage the energy and physical activity of our sons just as we expect our daughters to be quieter and more docile."[20]

From another part of the globe, Mary John Mananzan echoes the same experiences. Sadly but truly, she describes how sexual stereotyping is part of the process of socialization.

> "Right from a young age, even in nursery and kindergarten books, girls are encouraged to be clean, neat, tidy, tender little *charmers*, while boys are expected to be active, exploratory, rebellious and *mischievous*. Mothers are forever chiding daughters for being boisterous [boy-sterous]. Girls are enjoined to be quiet, sweet, pliable, coy, unobtrusive, 'lady-like' and feminine"[21]

Schools also reinforce stereotypical gender roles. Girls are expected to be more orderly and quiet than boys. Teachers expect—even tolerate—more deviant behaviour from boys than from girls.

Gradually, from the attitude of the adult members, the girl somehow absorbs the value that what is most important for her is *to be pretty*. She is *socialized* into spending most of her time, energy and money in making herself physically attractive. If people comment negatively on her looks she is hurt and feels demoralized. The multi-million dollar cosmetic industry is based on the "brainwashing" of all people—both men and women—that the most important thing for a girl is to be beautiful. Perhaps is this somehow connected with the idea that a girl has to attract a boy so she can fulfill her highest dream, which is to get married and be a wife and mother? The formation of a girl, whether it be in deportment, manner of dressing, speaking, attitude, skills or training is entirely geared to making her valuable in the marriage market.[22]

No doubt there are exceptions. There are many women—and their number is growing—who contest these stereotypes and fight this enforced socialization. They refuse to be intimidated by male comments on their looks. They continue to demonstrate that a woman will be regarded not just for her beauty, but for her intelligence, qualities of character and personality, for her courage and spirituality. Despite textbooks that show women only as nurses, teachers, social workers, counsellors and secretaries—there are many women who break frontiers and challenge stereotypes. They become lawyers, doctors, engineers and business managers.

In the Bible, in the book of Esther, we have the outstanding example of Queen Vashti (Esther 1:9-12). At one of the royal banquets, when King Ahasuerus had more than his share of wine, he sent for Queen Vashti and *commanded* that *she wear the royal crown* and present herself in the royal court *that all men might admire her beauty*. Queen Vashti refused the king's commands. She refused to "display" her beauty. Her defiance angered the king and he stripped her of her crown and of her queenship. Not that she cared. Queen Vashti was one example of a person who defied a sexual stereotype. Although no longer the queen of Ahasuerus, she still reigns as Queen in the hearts and minds of many women fighting against such sexual stereotypes.

9
The Story of Hagar
Symbol for Domestic Workers
ᦉ

Savitri, a young, attractive woman, originally from a rural area of Maharashtra, once came to the parish house and recounted her story. She had been working as a domestic in one of the upper middle class families of our city. Allegedly caught by her 'Memsahib' in a compromising position with the eldest son of the house, she had been abruptly thrown out of the house. Her vigorous protests "Your son made all the advances! I was absolutely powerless! It was not my fault!!" were all to no avail. Bundled out of the house, she found herself on the streets with her little bag in hand. From one point of view, she was glad to leave because life in that house meant continuous ill-treatment and verbal harassment. Every time she cooked a good dish and the Sahib praised her culinary skills, the Memsahib would look daggers at her. Madam would never leave her alone. One task after another, no rest, no holidays, no leave. And now, on the top of it all, this false charge. The problem was that she had no money and nowhere to go.

The story of Savitri reminds me of the story of Hagar in the book of Genesis. (Genesis 16:1-16 and 21:1-21). Hagar was the maidservant of Sarah, wife of Abraham. Sarah was barren, but the law permitted her to give her maidservant as a concubine to her husband, so that through her they could have 'legitimate' offspring. So Hagar was obliged to sleep with Abraham and promptly she conceived a child. At this point Sarah began to feel jealous. She complained to Abraham that Hagar looked down on her because of her barrenness and thus started to ill-treat the maidservant. Hagar decides to run away. She departs with her child, but on the way is visited by an angel of the Lord who tells her to go back. She relents and goes back. After a couple of years, the sterile Sarah gives birth to her own child, Isaac. Sarah now has no use for Hagar and forces Abraham to banish her. Hagar departs a second time into the desert. On the difficult journey, her child is about to die, when again an angel of the Lord visits her and gives her good news and hope for the future: "God has looked kindly on your son, Ishmael. He will live, become strong, be the founder of a great nation and will have many descendants!" Thus the story of Hagar, triply oppressed because she is a woman, a slave and a foreigner, ultimately ends on a note of hope that God will bring redress to the oppressed.

The story of Hagar brings to mind that it is not only the men who oppress women, but often it is the women themselves, who have absorbed patriarchal values, who oppress other women. Such was the nature of Sarah's ill treatment of Hagar.

Unfortunately, most of us tend to identify with Sarah and with Abraham and his dilemma. But if we re-read the story identifying with Hagar, we get a different point of view; we see her as a symbol and are occasioned to think of the plight of *all* domestic workers. Most of them are still referred to as "servants". Most of them are migrants, most are women, underpaid, subjected to long hours of work, with no job description, with no proper job contract, no leave, no holidays or periods of rest. Some of them are mere children, some are sexually harassed with no one to turn to for redress; the majority suffer verbal and physical abuse, harassment and mental cruelty.[23] *Like Hagar, they are objects, treated as objects and often discarded at the whim and fancy of their masters/*

mistresses. Their only source of hope, their only source of succour is their own solidarity.

In many cities of India house-workers' solidarities have been formed. Once a week they come together to meet other house-workers, study English, learn to read and write and, most importantly, share each other's problems and draw strength from their mutual experiences. The Biblical figure of Hagar is a symbol of the oppressed, exploited, rejected, homeless, accused, despised, powerless and helpless maidservant. But she is also a symbol of promise and hope because God stood by her side and fulfilled her wishes. She is the first person in the Bible to experience a divine encounter (visited twice by a messenger of God), the first woman mentioned to have borne a child and the only woman to receive a divine promise of descendants—which at that time and in that culture, when populations were dwindling, was one of the greatest blessings God could give a woman.

Hagar, a slave, became a child-bearer because of the law. So also it is by pressing for another law that we can enhance the self-image of all house-workers: *a law that will ultimately recognize them as workers*, thereby equal to all other workers in the eyes of the law, capable of all privileges, including the opportunity to petition the law courts and fight for their rights.[24] The challenge is to be the bearers of God's promise to all house-workers by mobilizing and advocating for such a law.

10
Naomi and Ruth
Sisters in Solidarity
ᘯ

In the experience of life's struggles, women often find themselves ranged or divided against each other: mother-in-law versus daughter-in-law; mistress of the house versus female domestic worker; female boss versus female secretary; brothel madam versus brothel prostitute. As a result, it is now become commonplace for the average 'unthinking' man to state that women are the cause of their own problems. So often we hear of cases of dowry harassment and the literature or media place the blame squarely on the mother-in-law for the harassment or torture of the new bride. So often we hear of domestic workers who are exploited or underpaid—and the blame is normally laid at the door of the mistress of the house. "The men in the house are kind and understanding," so it is reported, "but it is the mistress who cannot bear another woman being praised in her presence." In the offices, it is said that women are like cats. One secretary cannot tolerate another secretary being favoured over her by the boss.

And so the explanations go on. Quite often the author or writer is male. But even if the author is female, she is merely reproducing the thinking and mentality of the culture. What is often ignored is the fact that deep down, a woman is caught in a cycle of oppression and very often has no other option but to behave in the way she does. The thing to do is to break the cycle of oppression and for this there is only one solution—for women to come together in solidarity. That is why whenever we hear stories of women's solidarity, it is forever uplifting and heartening.[25] Such is the story of Naomi and Ruth.

In biblical society a woman was always dependent—on her father if unmarried, on her husband if married, and upon her adult son if widowed. So, if she was without father, without husband and without son, she was in a very pitiable state. Such was the status of Naomi and Ruth. When her husband Elimelech and his two sons died, Naomi was left in a foreign country with her Moabite daughters-in-law, Ruth and Orpah. She decides to go back to Judah and offers her daughters-in-law the choice of staying back in their native Moab. While Orpah stayed back, Ruth's decision was to remain with Naomi. Her famous declaration: "I will go where you go, and stay where you stay. Your people will be my people, your God will be my God!" can be transcribed very simply as: "Husbandless and childless, we are nobodies; only in solidarity can we survive!!"

Back in the land of Judah, Naomi shows Ruth that the only way to survive is to glean corn from the fields. There was a special law in Israel which allowed the poor, widows and orphans to gather the grain that the threshers dropped or passed over and keep what they had collected. (Lev 19:9-10,23:22, Deut. 24:19). Ruth becomes a gleaner and provides for both of them—enabling them to survive in this male dominated society.

Elimelech, Naomi's late husband did have some land in Judah, but the only way it could be redeemed was if Ruth bore a son, and Naomi had a grandson. Naomi next gives Ruth prudent advice on how to lure a husband. [This part of the story sounds almost like a seduction but is to be understood in its light-hearted romantic context]. Ruth does so—going to sleep late at night in the tent of

Boaz. Boaz, who is by now ensnared of her beauty, follows the levirate law and claims Ruth for his wife, thus redeeming the land for all three of them. Thus, the story ends happily, with the partnership in solidarity of Naomi and Ruth bearing fruit abundantly. Ruth and Boaz give birth to a son named Obed, who becomes the grandfather of David, the great king of Israel.

Thus, among the beautiful lessons we learn from this story is that if women combine, bond together and become sisters in solidarity, they have a way of getting out of their entrapment and slavery.

11
The Story of Abigail
Peacemaker in an Era of Violence
Ꮣ

May 11, 1998 was a day when several in the country burst firecrackers and gave in to wild rejoicing. India, they felt, had at last become a nuclear power. I wonder though if this is a matter for rejoicing. Nuclear power will not solve the myriad inequities India is now notorious for, among them the inequity between males and females. On the contrary, by going nuclear, India has only confirmed its status as a country where males continue to dominate and subordinate females. *Nuclearism* is just another expression of this patriarchal culture.

A 1999 survey in the city of Mumbai concluded that in resolving conflicts within the family, most women used discussion and verbal interaction, whereas a far greater proportion of men (in fact, almost double) were prone to use physical means of violence (beating, shoving, slapping, kicking or using an instrument to hurt women).[26]

Are men more violent than women? Some say that since men generally are physically stronger than women, they are accustomed to use physical means of violence to settle their problems. Others say that it is because of their socialization and training that men are brought up to think that it is all right to beat women.

While these considerations may be true, the deeper reason for the male attitude to violence against women however is to be found in the patriarchal attitude and patriarchal culture. This is a culture, which believes in graded hierarchical distinctions between groups. Once a classification is made, the next step is to understand one group as subordinate to the other. One chart of these graded distinctions[27] is as follows:

Male	Female
Master	Slave
Soul	Body
Rational	Emotional
Self-Confident	Need for Security
Aggressive, Rough	Gentle, Tactful

Once the dichotomy and hierarchical superiority is established, the obvious step is for males, who are more powerful, to want to subjugate and conquer the other half. Generally the instrument by which they do this is *force*—leading to the spiral of violence, militarizing, armaments, war and nuclear power. The military mindset stems from this 'will to dominate' and appears in all forms of violence: rape, torture, sexual abuse, incest, domestic violence, colonization and destruction of the earth. That is why historically, land and women were always considered as booty for the victorious army. That is why also, prostitution of women commonly accompanies military presence in a country.

The Biblical story of Abigail (I Samuel 25) provides a wonderful example of woman as peacemaker. David was trying to unify the tribes of Palestine and wanted Nabal, a rich sheepshearer, to be his ally. He sent messengers to Nabal asking that they be entertained with food and wine. Nabal rejected the invitation and refused hospitality to the messengers saying, "Who is David?" David was angry and wanted to destroy Nabal and his property. It would have led to a violent conflict in which many would have been killed. When Abigail, Nabal's wife, came to know of her husband's refusal and David's intent to destroy, she acted at once. Perceptive enough to realize that David was a great and specially anointed king she took provisions of bread, wine, fruit and grain and went out to meet David. She calmed David with her words, took the blame for her husband's brash insubordination and pacified him. David relented and decided not to attack. Abigail was the peacemaker between two warring and aggressive male egos.

Brian Easlea in his book, *Fathering the Unthinkable*, showed that nuclearism, in its ideology, language and imagery, is associated with masculinity strivings.[28] Males are the ones who militarize, colonialize, thirst for conquest and rape women of a captured country. If Easlea's analysis is true, one could very well ask if, while celebrating our nuclear status, we are celebrating our patriarchal culture as well—or worse, if while celebrating our power to explode bombs, we are celebrating our power to subordinate women as well?

12
The Story of Creation and the Fall
A Story of Subordination?

=== ᭳ ===

There are many myths regarding the story of "Creation and the Fall" in the Bible. Some of these need to be dispelled, because they can be a source of subordination of women.

Myth number 1: "There is only one *unique* story of creation."

Actually, the book of Genesis has two stories of creation, Genesis 1 and Genesis 2, and both of these have borrowed from the Babylonian legend of Enuma Elish. (Other religions too have their own stories of creation). Genesis 1 is the more recent story, written by priests, more logical and orderly. Genesis 2 is the more ancient account, more down-to-earth, attributed to the writer of the Yahwist tradition.[29] The fact that there are many stories goes to show that no one account is meant to be factual. They are complementary stories or legends, none of which are to be understood historically, but are all meant to convey a specific religious message.

Myth number 2: "Woman is inferior to man, because she was created from the rib of man" (Gen 2:21).

This myth does not consider the fact that the rib is only a symbol, and that too of equality. Verse 23 confirms that man and woman are equal, with the words: "This is bone of my bones, and flesh of my flesh" a Hebrew construction signifying equality. So, being created from the same rib, means being created in the same likeness, being created equally.[30]

Myth number 3: "Woman caused man to fall into sin. She is the temptress, the seductress, she is the one who collaborated with the serpent and caused man to eat the forbidden fruit."

This is perhaps the most destructive of all myths. The prevalence of this myth has been one of the causes for women all over the world to be beaten, raped, battered, corrected, reformed and brought into submission. According to this myth, man is originally good, but it is woman who sows evil thoughts and evil desires in his mind. Woman, by her very nature, seduces, tempts and leads man to sin. So, according to the myth, she has to be brought under control.[31] And when this myth further interprets the sin of disobedience as a sexual sin (for which there is absolutely no proof in the Bible) then we can understand why the idea that woman's body can be a source of temptation and why certain kinds of women like prostitutes, dancing women, and ill-clad women (even if because of poverty) are given such low moral status in our society!!

There is no doubt that the story of the Fall reflects the male Hebrew writer's strong sexist bias. Hebrew society at that time considered woman as man's property and therefore inferior to man. Hebrew laws were blatantly discriminatory towards women. The Biblical writers absorbed this bias. Even though there were several "Eve" stories that were circulating in the tradition at the time, the author of Genesis chose the most negative one.[32] There were other positive Eve stories; for instance the story which portrayed Eve, not as a seductress, but as one who helped Adam to become more fully aware of his consciousness. Had the author of Genesis incorporated this positive story about Eve, Christianity's whole attitude toward women may have been very different! The Hebrew writer deliberately left out such stories, because at that time in neighbouring Babylonian culture female goddesses and rituals were given great prominence. The author of Genesis did not want these practices to be followed in Israel.

Final question: So is the story of Adam and Eve true?

Answer: The story of Adam and Eve may not be true in the "historical" or "scientific" sense in which we understand the term today. In fact the Church holds that one can believe in Evolution without any discredit to the Bible. Nevertheless, the story of Adam and Eve, does convey a relevant message and briefly it is this: *That creation is good in itself, yet it is in the power of human beings, both men and women, to transform it for the better or for the worse.*

II

The Feminist Perspective and Contemporary Issues

13
Globalization

In the last few years a whole bevy of Indian women have been winning acclaim with their beauty. Sushmita Sen, Aishwarya Rai, Nafisa Joseph, Diana Hayden, Yukta Mukhi, Lara Dutta, Priyanka Chopra, etc. have either won the Miss Universe/Miss World titles or else have figured in the top ranks. I was asking myself: "Does this mean that Indian women have suddenly become beautiful or does this mean that the world at large has suddenly discovered Indian beauty?" I believe that neither is true. I believe that what is true is that the Western Cosmetic Industry has now discovered a market among the Indian middle classes and what better way to propagate a product than to subliminally convey a message to these classes that "You too can become rich, famous and beautiful like the models mentioned above if only you start wearing L'Oreal, Revlon, Amway or Oriflame products. . . ."

Not only the cosmetic industry, but the whole consumer industry has now been swamped with items like Pepsi, Coke, Kentucky Fried Chicken, McDonald's burgers; shirts from Louis Vitton, Jean Phillipe, Peter England and Van Heusen; detergents like soap and soap powder, and even toothpaste and toilet articles have begun to inundate the Indian market with foreign brand names and foreign products. The middle classes are lapping it all up.

This is one aspect of the phenomenon called liberalization. Liberalization means the opening up of markets, implying that foreign companies can now come into India and make consumer products. Liberalization itself is one aspect of globalization, the process by which transnational corporations are now free to operate anywhere on the globe.

An important effect of globalization is that it is making the lowest classes poorer than they were before. Mostly it is the women who are affected. As smaller firms are swallowed up by Multinationals or Transnationals, many women lose their jobs. They are offered the voluntary retirement scheme or the 'golden handshake'. Now that Transnationals are taking over the economy, traditional occupations that are farming or fishing related have also become obsolete. Deprived of their livelihood, many rural women are forced to migrate to the cities and take up jobs in the unorganized sector as domestic workers.[33] The advent of tourism and the five star culture has inducted women into avenues of waitressing and prostitution.

Another disastrous effect of globalization is called the *McDonaldization of culture*.[34] By this I do not refer to the advent of fast food restaurants in India, but to the bombardment of Western values on Indian TV channels through Western programmes like MTV, talk-shows, soap-operas, sit-coms, serials or movies—and with it the whole First World value-system of consumerism, materialism, profit seeking and success at any cost, etc. Even worse are the advertisements where women are often projected on the TV screen as "objects".

In all developing countries women have become pawns at the mercy of the forces of globalization and liberalization. In the Bible too there are many instances where women are treated as objects or as pawns. The story of Susanna (Daniel 13), at the mercy of the two wicked elders, in the book of Daniel is a typical example. Susanna, falsely accused by two wicked male judges, became a helpless pawn at the mercy of their lust, position and power. She was saved however by the wisdom of a young man named Daniel, who convicted them through their own lies.

Women today can be saved by their own wisdom—by an awareness that they are not objects of fate, but "subjects" of their own destiny. Women's organizations and women's movements, in the form of *Mahila Mandals*, are sprouting up all over the country and taking an active part in issues like rising prices, sexual discrimination, wife beating, dowry harassment, representation in the Panchayat, and most recently, the Women's Reservation Bill. Gradually we are witnessing the surge of women's empowerment and the political consciousness of women. It is these small micro movements like the women's movement and the ecological movement that have started a process that can counter the forces of globalization. Is this not perhaps a sign that the Holy Spirit is still present and active in the world?

14
The Environment: Eco-feminism
ઝ

In the outskirts of the city of Mumbai, a group of high
school students were animatedly discussing a
problem. The problem concerned a serious choice
facing the residents of a little seaside village. A plan had
been mooted to build a huge five star hotel by the seaside.
The group was divided over the issue. Some were in
favour of the five star hotel arguing that it would bring
the depressed area much needed money, a lot of jobs,
hordes of tourists and ultimately would change the
economy of the village. Others were against the new
construction saying that the hotel and the tourists would
not only destroy their agricultural land and crops but
that the tourists would pollute the seashore. What struck
me about the two groups was that those in favour of
preserving the environment and against the five star hotel
were predominantly females.

I was wondering why this is so. All over the world
women are very much a part of the ecological movement,
the Green movement, the movement to save the earth.
In India, Medha Patkar, has been the leader of the
Narmada Bachao Andolan. The agitation to save the
eastern seashore of India from prawn cultivators is also
spearheaded by women. Even the Chipko movement in
the north became a powerful movement because of the
presence in it of women. Is it because women feel a
great sympathy with Mother Earth? Is it because the
rape of the land has been likened to the rape of a woman?

No doubt there are striking parallels, which exist between the treatment of the Earth and the treatment of women. For instance, both women and the Earth are seen in terms of their *usefulness* rather than as having intrinsic worth in their own right. Both are made to occupy a subordinate position in the hierarchical system; women are subordinated to men and nature is subordinated to human beings. This coming together of ecology and feminism, by those who see the link between the domination of women and the domination of nature, is called *Eco-feminism*. It is a movement which is now gathering force all over the world, is spiritual in nature and perceives parallels between women and nature on the conceptual level as well— the level of world view, myth, symbol, idea and image.

Very often people who are in favour of indiscriminate building, killing animals, destroying land or trees and ravaging nature quote the book of Genesis 1:28 where God is said to have told the first inhabitants to "till the earth and *subdue it and have dominion. . . over every living thing*". They argue that God himself gave the command to subdue and "conquer" the earth. They forget that this text was written in a time of exile and the real meaning is that the author was trying to give the dejected Israelites hope and encouragement that they could go back and re-construct a land that had been devastated by war and neglect. They forget that there is another text in Genesis 2:15, actually earlier in origin, which says that "God placed humans in the garden of Eden to *cultivate it and be stewards of it*". Hence to use the text of Genesis 1:28 to justify plundering the earth's resources is to make a mockery of the meaning and intent of God's command.[35]

Eco-feminism is more than a political alliance between two groups promoting a common cause; rather it is based on the recognition that the reacquisition of "*feminist styles of thinking and being*" are the very means by which environmental sanity can be restored. The exploitative, energy-consuming, individualistic habits of Western culture must be replaced by a nurturing, cooperative, communal way of being that is rooted in real connectedness to other humans and the earth. Eco-feminism is more than an attitude. It is a lifestyle, a way of living that is conscious of wasting non-renewable energies and resources of the earth.

There is also an 'ecology of the world within our bodies'. Philosophers like Ricoeur believe that the cosmic spirit is one with the spirit within our bodies.[36] Ecological thinking therefore stresses the need to respect the natural system of our bodies. The ideal would be to "design with nature" and not to force human designs upon it. Health is not the absence of disease; health is what happens when a complexly balanced system runs smoothly. The correct way to treat disease—like the correct way to treat ecological problems of erosion or tree blight—is not to attack the immediate cause, but to restore the system's depressed ability to resist. The pesticide and the bulldozer, chemical medicine and the scalpel; these only remove the symptoms of ill health. Awareness of healthy foods, the shunning of whatever it is that pollutes life (gases, liquids or solids), alternative therapies and a return to simple living in harmony with nature—all of this reflects a distinctive ecological way of thinking.

Feminist spirituality is very much in keeping with Eco-spirituality, the *spirituality of the modern era*. It is an outlook which is respectful of all life, not just human life. It is a viewpoint which is humble and realizes that humans are only a tiny fraction of the universe. It is a perspective which is found in all religions, not just the biblical religion. It is an attitude, which is found in Psalms 104, 148 and in the poem of St. Francis of Assisi:

"Be praised, O Lord, for brother Wind
And for the air cloudy and clean,
By which you give substance to your creatures,
Be praised, O Lord, for our sister, *Mother Earth*,
who sustains and governs us
And produces fruits with colourful leaves and flowers."

15
Morality: Private or Public?

ℭ

The newspapers in the month of September, 1998 were full of Bill Clinton's extra marital affair with Monica Lewinsky. In the Sunday Times of Sept. 14, 1998 a few prominent Indians, like a filmmaker, a photographer and a singer were interviewed and were asked their opinion as to what they felt about it. Some of them seemed to say that "So long as he is a good President, who cares about his secret, private life? So long as he is effective in his ruling of the country, it does not matter one bit what he does in his private, personal life!" I wonder if we can accept this kind of separation of private and public life, this kind of dichotomy between the personal and the political.

The purpose of this article is not to sit in judgement over Clinton or to question his motives. That is not our prerogative. I would agree also that the affair has been over-hyped, over-exposed and far too publicized. Here I merely wish to discuss a moral principle. *Can morality be purely private*? Is it purely a question between the individual and his God? Aren't others affected? Aren't Monica and her family affected? Aren't Hillary, Clinton's wife, and Chelsea, his daughter, also affected?

Those who make a separation between private and public morality—appear to be saying that ethics and the commandments are only for one's personal life. With regard to public life there is no morality, there is only "efficiency" and "effectiveness".

If someone tells lies about his private life, what is to prevent him from telling lies also in his public life. In other words, if Clinton has lied about his personal life, surely he must be expected to lie also about the United States' relations with China and India. The private sphere is connected to the public. It is like a seamless garment. Surely, if we cannot trust a person with regard to his private life, much less will we able to trust him with regard to his public life.

Then there is the whole question of the Presidential role model. If leaders and public figures offer these kinds of values, what can we expect of the youth and children? The youth will have no ideals, no heroes, no values to live by. There will be a huge, gaping hole in their formation.

This is the situation in India. It is precisely because we make a separation between the private and the public life, that we have so many persons who will publicly and religiously visit temple, mosque or church and even give donations, but in their secret private lives they are criminals, involved in scams, and corrupt to the core.

It is for this reason that Feminists do not accept this division between the personal and the political.[37] Chauvinistic males would love to maintain such a dichotomy so that the man's role is reserved for the public sphere of economics and politics, while the woman's role is relegated to the private sphere of the household. Patriarchal culture would like to keep these two spheres apart so that in this way women are restricted to the sphere of the home and rendered powerless and unable to transform the significant structures of public society. Capitalists and politicians too would like to preserve this division of the private and the public. Since morality, they believe, is a private thing between you and your God, moral and ethical ideals are not supposed to overflow into their public life; thus they cannot be publicly censured for their illegal, illicit and unethical business and political practices.

For Jesus, morality was integral and holistic. There was no separation between the private and the public. That's why he openly attacked the Pharisees for their hypocrisy and legalism, he candidly challenged the priestly class for their exploitation of the temple for mercenary profit. These were "public" unethical practices. At the same time Jesus also decried the false intention and false motive behind external, ritual actions. Morality as taught by Jesus is both private and public, personal and political. Only this holistic understanding of morality can make for the creation of a new humanity.

16
Fundamentalism and Women
❧

One of the most shocking stories in the Old Testament is the story of Jepthah and his daughter (Judges 11). Jepthah, a military leader, led his people against the Ammonites. As he went into battle, he extracted a promise from God. "If you make me victorious," he vowed, "on my return from war, I will sacrifice whoever or whatever I encounter as I come out of my house!" Jepthah was victorious, but unfortunately the first person he met on his return was his own daughter. Jepthah was sad that he had to do away with his only daughter, but determined to be true to his vow, he killed her. The poor girl had no choice or say of her own. She is a hapless victim, sacrificed to the "reified" tenet of a fundamentalist religion. When a religious tenet—be it a vow or ritual, doctrine or law—is made into an absolute, so much so that persons are made subservient to it, then we have the phenomenon of "reification". Things are made more important than persons.[38] Jepthah was a sincere man, but he had the beginnings of a fundamentalist way of thinking. He made the law into an 'absolute'. Unfortunately, such ways of thinking do not belong only to Old Testament times. They are very much a phenomenon of our times as well.

In April 1999 a 29-year-old Pakistani woman was murdered in broad daylight because *Muslim* fundamentalists thought that she had dishonoured the community by seeking a divorce from her abusive husband. In 1992,

Hindu fundamentalists in India, seeking to preserve ground which they considered sacred, attacked the Babri Masjid, and let loose a wave of communal riots, which caused havoc to life, limb and property in which women were the greatest victims. Similarly, modern *Christian* fundamentalists, interpreting St. Paul in a very literal and non-real sense, strongly advocate that wives should submit to their husbands, cover their heads, keep silent in church and give up their jobs. In all these cases, people, especially women, are sacrificed to the whims and fancies of "absolute" religious tenets.

What is fundamentalism? And why does it seek to repress women in particular? Religious fundamentalism is a pattern of belief and behaviour, which has emerged within the last 25 years in all the major religions of the world, Christianity, Islam, Judaism and Hinduism. It is characterized by a 'literal' understanding of the Scriptures and a fanatic devotion to religious tenets, which have assumed the nature of absolutes. Some have called fundamentalism an ideology, others have called it a movement, but the different fundamentalist groups within each religion are all very unique. However, one common characteristic that fundamentalists all over the world share is that they feel *threatened*. They are afraid that their entire world, their entire system of values is collapsing under the impact of modern, rational culture. Hence, they fight back vigorously and cling to their absolutes in seeking to preserve their 'traditional' world.

Another common characteristic of fundamentalists is the *control of gender relations*. Because fundamentalists are not in a position to reverse urbanization, modernization, industrialization and other global forces, they focus on the family. By forcing women to live behind the *chadar* (veil) and behind the *chardivari* (four walls), they seek to order gender relations along traditional or patriarchal lines. Fundamentalists have a concept of family which is pre-modern. When they speak of restoring the family,

5. Dare to see...

they mean restoring hierarchical relations: men in charge, women obeying and submitting. Men are the bread-winners; women have to look after children and home.[39]

Given the fact that women have to relinquish their power and authority to men, *why do women join fundamentalist groups?* The Harvard Professor Helen Hardacre gives several reasons, the most important being that fundamentalism gives woman a sense of status. According to the fundamentalist worldview, woman is the carrier of tradition; she is in charge of the home, responsible for the happiness and well-being of everyone in it. Excluded from the labour force, the only way she can live at a higher standard and gain status is by being coupled with a man. Hence, women who join fundamentalist groups are "happy" to be subservient to their husbands.[40]

The gospels portray Jesus giving a very different message. Through his actions and words, he decried ritualism and fundamentalism. Seven times the gospels report him as performing a miracle on the Sabbath. "The Sabbath is made for people, not people for the Sabbath" were his words. The early Christians and St Paul continued this protest against the absolutism of the law and the discrimination against women. The baptismal confession "And now there are no more distinctions between us, between Jew and Greek, slave and free person, male and female." (Gal. 3:28) bears this out.[41] Pope John Paul II following the same tradition wrote a beautiful Apostolic letter in which he spoke of the dignity and equality of women. "Both man and woman are human beings to an equal degree, because both are created [equally] in God's image." (*Mulieris Dignitatem, # 6*)

17
Women's Spirituality

— ᧁ —

Spirituality means allowing oneself, one's life to be taken over by the Spirit. The initiative comes from the Spirit. On our part, we can only take away the obstacles, the hurdles that block the Spirit from taking over our lives.

For males, the main block that prevents the Spirit from taking over their lives is pride, a sense of one's self-importance, an urge to dominate others, a form of self-elevation. Protestant theologians Reinhold Neibuhr and Paul Tillich have described this pride or 'hubris' in great detail so much so that they have understood the sin of Adam and Eve to be a sin of pride.

Women theologians however feel that this is not women's experience. For women, the main block to spirituality is the 'opposite' of pride. It is the *sin of hiding*. Women tend to self-abnegate themselves, to depend totally on others, to consider themselves inadequate, to give importance to others. And this is what blocks their spiritual growth.[42]

Hence, one aspect of developing women's spirituality is to fight against that sin by which women are led to think that they are unimportant, by which women denigrate themselves, by which they give precedence to others. If spirituality consists in overcoming those obstacles that alienate us from spiritual growth, then spirituality for women consists in developing their independence and getting rid of anything that advocates a subordinate role for them. Two such areas of women's subjugation are work and worship.

Work: One area which forces women into a subordinate role is the segregated job market. This is the job market by which one stream directs men to all the top executive, managerial jobs and another stream directs women to all the subordinate, secondary jobs. Thus women are encouraged to be secretaries, nurses, teachers, counsellors, administrative assistants, legal aides and social workers, while men are encouraged to be bosses, doctors, principals, managers, presidents, lawyers and directors of social work agencies. In the Church too, women are persuaded to be para-liturgical assistants and parish secretaries while men are allowed to become theologians or Scripture scholars. This then is one area which is a hindrance to women's full spiritual development and so directing young women to take up a particular type of education or profession is a crucial element in the shaping of women's spirituality.

Worship: Another area which can play an important part in reinforcing this subordinate role of women is the liturgy. We all believe that the liturgy is a significant part of our spiritual lives. We listen to the liturgical readings every week and often several times in the week. Unfortunately, if we look at the liturgical readings we find that women characters play a very subordinate or shadow role. Theologian Margaret Proctor-Smith made a study of the 772 texts in the *Common Lectionary* and found that only 14.7 percent had significant references to women. Another 6 percent had peripheral references.[43] Thus, women are included in the readings only in so far as they relate to male characters, not regarded as actors in their own rights. Mostly they are appendages and expendable. Sarah, for instance, is included in the reading only in as much as she relates to Abraham.

It could be argued that women in the Biblical era are not very visible and the Bible simply reflects this regrettable fact. But if it is the function of the liturgy to be *selective* rather than *representative*, then we need to make a special effort to recall and celebrate those women in whom the Spirit has been made manifest and through whom the Spirit has worked in special ways. Thus, whenever there is a chance to choose liturgical readings, every opportunity should be taken to promulgate the stories of Rebekah, Rachel and Leah, Miriam and Deborah, Esther and Judith, Abigail and Vashti, Shiprah and Puah, Naomi and Ruth, Mary, Mary Magdalene, Aquila, Nympha, Phoebe and other women leaders/ heroines.

By focusing on the stories of these women, the world is given newer models and newer images of spirituality. Today, all over the world, but especially in developing countries, women's spirituality and women's leadership is burgeoning forth in many different ways and spheres of life. And there is so much that the world can learn from them: attitudes of compassion, creative images, newer 'care taking' styles of leadership, concern for Nature and the human body, respect for life. Mary Jo Weaver, speaking for all women, put it succinctly when she said: "If spirituality is a hunger, then we are simply famished!"[44]

18
The Peace Movement
The Real Hijacking
❧

In the last week of 1999, when the rest of the world was preparing to usher in the New Millennium, India was battling with a hijack crisis that promised all the signals of a violent ending. Ironically, when most of the world was celebrating the start of the International Year of Peace, India was struggling to negotiate with militant terrorists to save the lives of 150 passengers, who had been hijacked to Kandahar.

Why did this happen? Why was India caught in such a vice-like grip? The real crisis, I believe, began much earlier with the hijacking of the peace movement. What is the peace movement? Since the last 10 years or so, as part of the preparations for the 50th anniversary of the Independence of India and Pakistan, there has been a stirring within the peoples of the two countries of a genuine desire for peace. This mass-based movement, called the *Pakistan-India People's Forum*, originated *not* from the governments, but from the members of civil society. This Forum, made up of intellectuals, activists, journalists and peace-loving peoples, had already met on several occasions, in Lahore, in Delhi and in Calcutta, had set in motion a gradual movement among the peoples of Pakistan and India and was making vast strides towards the goal of long-lasting peace between the two countries.

Peace can only be an initiative of peoples, an initiative of the masses. The problem is that the few, the oligarchy,

70

manipulate the masses for their own political reasons, work on them emotionally and get them all geared up for war and aggression. This is what Hitler did. This is what all Fascists do. In actual practice, the common man or woman does not want war. If you make a survey of the people of Pakistan, you will find that 99 out of 100 persons do not want a war with India. Yet, a few persons, notably those with military inclinations, take a decision for the majority and then churn up the people's emotions in antagonism toward 'the other country, the enemy'. Similarly, if you make a survey of the population of India, you will find that 99% of the people (if not more) did not want to attack the Babri Masjid. Yet again, it was a few people, who whipped up a hate campaign and incited the 'kar sevaks' to attack the mosque. Decisions to make a nuclear bomb, decisions to attack a mosque, decisions to terrorize cannot come out of the discussion of a *public* forum. These are decisions taken by a few people. They are not part of the desire or will of the common people. It is these decisions that have hijacked the peace movement.

At the world level too, the same phenomenon of the 'rule of the few' has been repeated. In May 1999, the United Nations had planned a World Conference on Peace at the Hague in the Netherlands, but unfortunately it was not to be. The Conference fell through because of the lack of governmental support. The elite who make up the governments of this world did not want peace. However, the assembly of the peoples of the world, the NGOs and all those who make up civil society, came together, organized a People's Conference on Peace at the Hague itself and made a number of concrete and relevant decisions.[45]

A similar thing happened in Palestine 2000 years ago. The Jesus movement was a movement that had caught the imagination of all people of low status—the lepers, the outcastes, the tax collectors, the prostitutes, the peasants, the blind, deaf and crippled. They were all willing to go along with Jesus to the "ends of the earth." Unfortunately the leaders of the Sanhedrin pitted Jesus, a peace-loving prophet, against Barabbas, a militant zealot, who wanted to overthrow the Romans with violence. The leaders incited the people *against Jesus* so that when Pilate asked them to make that fateful choice, they opted for Barabbas. Again, it was a few, who had manipulated the many. After the death of Jesus however, the apostles came together and re-started the movement of love, justice and non-violence.

Religion preaches peace, love and openness. Yet, if we look around the world today, we find so many religious wars generating hatred—Ireland, Bosnia, Iraq, Chechnya, Timor, Sri Lanka, India. Why is this so? Partly because underlying these wars are socio-economic factors; partly because religion, which is capable of evoking powerful emotions, has been "hijacked" for political reasons and what is mouthed as religion is only a veneer of it.

We are living today in a war culture. Our vocabulary, terminology and expressions are all war-related. Words like 'contest' 'compete' 'vanquish' 'victor' 'defeat' 'destroy' 'bombard' 'blast' are taken for granted. Even sports is advertised as though it were a war between two teams. This culture of war, sadly, camouflages the real problems that lie underneath.

This culture of war, this military mind-set, this desire to be aggressive and overpowering is all part of a patriarchal culture, which bases itself on the hierarchical superiority of males over females. A feminist culture, on the other hand, which desires equality in relationships, is a peace-loving culture. Unfortunately however, women, by the mere fact of being women, do not necessarily possess peace-loving attitudes. In fact, many women have absorbed the patriarchal attitudes of the surrounding culture and, as a result, ignore or neglect the more pressing, underlying problems of their family or nation.

In her brilliant story *A Coincidence*, Ahmed Nadeem Quasmi, tells of a middle class woman, who plans to get her daughter married off, and borrows furniture, upholstery, curtains and fineries to deck up her drawing room in a bid to impress the mother of the future groom. This woman however, when she visits, probes the interior and discovers the miserable condition of her would-be-in laws. Instead of taking umbrage she breaks into laughter for she herself has also a borrowed a huge limousine to impress her prospective daughter-in-law's mother. The story has a useful moral. India and Pakistan, like the two women, have borrowed robes—the expensive plumage of military hardware—which they need to vie with each other and engage in mutual sabre-rattling. But behind these extravagant displays of rivalry, the backyards of both nations resemble each other in poverty and misery. Are we going to continue this "monumental frippery" or are we going to take stock, laugh at ourselves and begin the genuine movement for Peace?

19
God: Father or Mother?
Women and Divinity
ᡍ

Recently a young couple approached me and said, "I know that we have been accustomed to calling God 'Our Father'. But *can we also call God 'Our Mother? Can we refer to God as a She?"* I found their question very relevant since the year 1999 had been dedicated to God the Father. Their question introduces the whole issue of God as Feminine.

Whenever we speak of God we use what is called 'analogy'. This means that all discourse about God is *partly true and partly untrue.* Thus for instance, when we say God is Father, it is true that certain positive qualities of Fatherhood are implied, but it is also true that God is not a father, in the sense that He does not have the limitations of a human father. In point of fact, God is sexless; neither male nor female. But our tradition has attributed certain roles to 'Him', predominantly male roles, like Father, Ruler, King, Husband, Son, Bridegroom, Shepherd. What we tend to forget is that all our language is analogical and all these metaphors are only partly true.

It is true that we tend to become like the God in whom we believe. If so, then our use of all-male designations and symbols to describe the deity will certainly make a difference to the way we shape our lives. In the history of Western art, the most common depiction of God is that of an old man with a white beard. The power of these images is to subliminally suggest that our God is literally male. Further, they imply that every man, like the male-God, is the 'ruler' of home, family, polity and society. As a result, such images at the same time, denigrate woman's dignity.

How then should we speak of God? Elizabeth Johnson categorizes three distinct approaches to speaking about God in an inclusive way:[46]

1. *One way* is to emphasize the feminine traits of God. To say that God, though Father, is compassionate, kind, loving, motherly, caring, etc and to emphasize those passages where God's feminine traits are mentioned. For instance, Is 49:15 "Though a mother forget her sucking child, or have no compassion on the child of her womb, yet I will not forget you!" or Lk 13:34 "Jerusalem, Jerusalem, how many times have I wanted to put my arms around all your people, just as a hen gathers her chicks under her wings, but you would not let me."

2. *The second way* is to speak of a feminine dimension in the Godhead. This feminine principle is generally associated with the Holy Spirit. There are several grounds for associating the Holy Spirit with the maternal function of God. In the book of Genesis, the Spirit is referred to as *ruah*, which is a feminine noun. Further, the functions of the Holy Spirit are those of *giving birth:* to the world, (Creation in Genesis), to Jesus (through conception in Mary), and to the Church (at Pentecost). Other functions are preserving, sustaining, assisting (being a Paraclete), nurturing, educating, inspiring, counselling. There was a Semitic and Syrian tradition in early history which spoke of this feminine principle in the Godhead, but when the male-dominated Greco-Roman culture superimposed itself on this early tradition, this insight was lost.

In both these attempts God remains essentially male, but now tempered by the ideal feminine so that believers need not rebel against a crushing paternalism. The feminine is incorporated in a subordinate way into an overall symbol that still remains essentially masculine.

3. *A third way* is to speak of God using *inclusive* images, using *both male and female images*. This is the preferred way. Thus we would balance images of God as Father, King, Shepherd, Bridegroom with images of God as Mother, Midwife, Nurse, Shepherdess, Mistress. A striking example is found in Luke 15, where the shepherd is looking for his lost sheep with the parallel parable of the homemaker searching for her lost coin.

According to the analytical psychiatrist, C. G. Jung, it is difficult for men and women to achieve psychological integrity without an archetype of the feminine in God.[47] Not only women, but men also, are crippled by this all male image of God. To be whole persons, men need to complement their masculine traits with the feminine.

I cannot help believing that a lot of the violence against women in the world (eve-teasing, rape and battering) is due partly to an all-male concept of God. To come back then to the question posed to me by the young couple, my answer would be: "Not only are we allowed to call God our Mother, but every prayer instead of beginning, 'God, our Father', should preferably begin 'God, our Father and Mother'." Not for nothing does theologian Elizabeth Johnson title her book on God as "She Who Is!"

20
Does Mass Media Degrade the Image of Women?
ॐ

Imagine these two scenarios: **Scenario A**: An advertisement for a mattress where a young woman is portrayed reclining 'Venus like' in a scanty diaphanous nightgown and the man looks longingly at her. The implication is that buying the mattress will buy you sensuality. **Scenario B**: A box office movie where the female heroine, equally young, repulses the advances of her romantic suitors at her work place, then gets married to her boss and becomes a housewife who cooks, cleans, dusts and scrubs the house. The implication is that a good moral, ethical housewife is one who is a stay-at-home mother.

The obvious question that comes to mind then is: Which of the two scenarios is more offensive? which of the two is more degrading to the image of a woman? An advertisement, which reveals the anatomy of a woman, or a story, which straitjackets women into cramped, stereo-typical roles? While scenario A is struck off by the censors and dubbed as obscene, because it portrays woman as a sex-object, scenario B passes the censors even though it is actively promoting a cultural stereotype and casting woman into a specific and very restrictive role.

It is this kind of double standard that women are objecting to. While they are definitely against the portrayal of women as sex objects, they are likewise against the casting of women into roles that support patriarchy. In an earlier era, the protest was against textbooks that represented women solely in roles such as nurses, teachers, social workers, secretaries, air stewardesses, beauty stylists in other service-oriented jobs. Today students of gender studies not only highlight how the media objectify women but they also uncover how the media is partial and biased in its portrayal of women.

Take the TV coverage of the Kargil issue for example. Uma Chakravarti has pointed out that prominent among the scenes flashed on the screen were those of strong young soldiers who withstood the cold and the hardships of the Siachen glacier, as well as the onslaught of the Pakistani forces. Side by side however were scenes of their corpses being brought home to their weeping, wailing wives. In other words, the subliminal implication is that while the young male jawans gave their blood for the country on the tops of mountains, the sentimental, sobbing females stayed at home and looked after house and children.[48]

Perhaps a bigger blow to the image of women on the TV screen is the near-absence, disappearance or exclusion of a particular category of woman from TV shows. With the dominance of the private channels, Star TV, Zee TV, Sony, Max, Sahara, etc the image being thrown at us in the advertisements, serials and chat shows is the **image** of the glossy, **urban, upper class housewife.** Speaking Hindi with the odd English word thrown in between, this urban, upper class woman is the target of consumer products for her spruced-up kitchen, sitting room, garden or car. What is ignored is the concept that this urban woman may have interests other than cooking utensils and washing machines; what has dropped out of view completely is the context and life of rural India and its rural women. The only time village India and village women are shown on the screen is when there is a calamity or disaster or when her simple life is 'exoticized' in National Geographic.[49]

The worst kind of degradation to the image of women is the complete silencing or censorship of authors and artists who write on issues affecting women. The banning of Taslima Nasreen's book 'Lajja' or the boycott of Deepa Mehta's movies 'Fire' and 'Water' or the banning of Vijay Tendulkar's plays 'Sakharam Binder' and 'Ghashiram Kotwal' are cases in point.

One excuse given by the market-driven publishers and theatre-owners is that women's stories are stories of particular groups, of local areas; they do not have universal appeal; they are stories of minorities, which would not appeal to the majority. The other reason given by the Fundamentalists and the Saffron Brigade is that these stories are a 'blight' on Indian culture. Isn't it ironic that on the very day the Bajrang Dal violently stopped the shooting of 'Water' (because it reported the sad stories of Indian widows), the newspapers carried an item about an eleven-year-old girl being forcibly married to a much older man? Strangely, the Bajrang Dal had no protest to make against this forced child-marriage, which is a far bigger blight on Indian culture.

If we turn to Church circles too, there is great scope for more equal relations. Saints in our liturgical calendar are like media models of sanctity. There are, in the calendar, approximately 130 feast days reserved for male saints and only 36 reserved for females, 12 of which are reserved for Mary. In short, there are just 24 female saints.[50] This of course does not mean that women are less saintly than men, but it does imply that the Church reflects the values of the surrounding society and that the feminization of the Church has still a long way to go.

21
Countering the Demon of Ageism
⸙

When she was in her late fifties, my mother often heard the comment "I can't believe that you are that old. You don't look that old!". At other times, people would say something like "You remind me of my grandmother!" or "Will you be able to climb those stairs?" Somehow these statements, mostly innocuous and meant to show concern, are actually very patronizing for an older woman and make her feel somewhat diminished or labelled. 1999 was declared the "Year of the Elderly" and, at the start of the new millennium, we need perhaps to take a fresh look at the problem of ageing.

Nowadays, we often hear the expression "the greying" of the population, meaning that substantial proportions of the population are aged 60 years and above. At present, the proportion of aged people in India is 7.59 percent.[51] However, in absolute numbers, this works out to approximately 100 million, which is larger than the population of most countries in Europe. Further, in India, we hardly have any facilities or resources to take care of our aged people, as they have in Europe and America. Hence, the ageing of our population is a big problem.

The second remarkable characteristic of the ageing population is that the greater proportion is made up of women. 'Oh yes!' we say with some degree of pride "our women outlive our men, our women are tougher than men!" But the real question is: what is the quality of life of these older women? Most of them suffer from ill-health:

osteoporosis, cardiovascular and pulmonary diseases, hypertension, diabetes, Parkinson's, senility—a result of the stresses and strains of their earlier home-caring, child-bearing years. Many of these elder women are living in poverty, many are widows, most of them are uncared for, ignored, forgotten, invisible, neglected, devalued, treated as irrelevant and peripheral. How come we have such a totally denigrating picture of old women?

The saddest thing is that they are subjects of a subtle discrimination. They are valued in society only in as much as they are young and "beautiful", in as much as they are productive, and in as much as they are valuable to men. This is ageism or the 'systematic stereotyping and discrimination against people because they are old'. Ageism is inextricably tied to sexism. Look at some of the cultural stereotypes in Western literature. In children's stories, it is often old women who personify malevolence, as 'old hags', evil crones and scary old witches. The ageing queen witch in Snow White, the old witch in Hansel and Gretel, the wicked stepmother in Cinderella are all old women who threatened to harm or even kill youngsters. Thus, children as well as adults grow up learning to scorn old maids and calling someone an 'old woman' is an insult.[52]

The real challenge to counter 'ageism' is to recognize older women for their true worth and value, enabling them to keep their sense of self-esteem. Actually, there are many societies where the older woman is respected both politically and religiously—matriarchal societies, the Western Australian aborigines, the Canadian plain Indians, China and Japan before the Revolution and in West Africa before the advent of Western colonizers. In the Bible too there are quite a few instances where an older woman is respected for her wisdom or her caring qualities. In Luke 2, we read of Anna the prophetess, in Acts 9:36-42, we hear of the widows of Joppa respecting Dorcas, the seamstress, but the best example is of Huldah the prophet in 2 Kings:22.

81

In the seventh century BCE, King Josiah led a campaign to initiate reforms in Israel. During his reign, an ancient scroll was discovered in the temple. The king commissions his high priest and top officers to ascertain whether the scroll is authoritative. The five men look for a prophet to discern this. Despite the availability of several male prophets living nearby at the time—Jeremiah, Zephaniah, Nahum, the royal delegation turns instead to the elder woman, Huldah (probably because she was literate). The cabinet officials go to Huldah's home to confer with her and they accept without question her right to pronounce judgement. She verifies that the scroll contains God's message and then provides an interpretation. Scholars now agree that the Jerusalem woman had actually certified the core of the book of Deuteronomy. That day in 621 BCE Huldah did a momentous thing. Until then, no writings had ever been declared to be Holy Scripture. She became the first Scripture authority and the founder of Biblical studies.[53]

Twenty-six centuries ago, King Josiah and his officials recognized wisdom in an older woman. They give us an outstanding example for our era. Like the British-American poet Astra, (an extract from whose poem 'Older and Bolder' is quoted below, with a slight modification) they proclaim that women get wiser and bolder as they get on in years.

Wiser and bolder as I get older,
I'll do as I choose—what's there to lose?
too long I've been dutiful, told to look beautiful,
diverted with sweet talk or threats when I'd try to balk,
but now I can show them, how I can throw them,
by turning the tables, discarding all labels, hag, nag
    and bag.
cause as I get older, I'm wiser and bolder
what's there to lose? I'll do as I choose.

22
AIDS: The New Scourge of Women
೮

Within a decade, it is expected that, India will have the dubious distinction of being the World's AIDS capital, having the largest number of reported HIV cases in the world.[54] Even though the prevalence rate may not be the highest, India has, in absolute numbers, the largest number of HIV infected cases in Asia (see table below)

Table: Estimates of Adult HIV Infections

Country	Number	Percent Prevalence
India	**4,100,000**	**0.80**
Thailand	770,000	2.23
Myanmar	440,000	1.79
China	400,000	0.06
Cambodia	120,000	2.40
Vietnam	86,000	0.06
Malaysia	66,000	0.62
Pakistan	62,000	0.09
Indonesia	51,000	0.05
Nepal	25,000	0.24
Philippines	23,000	0.06
Japan	6,800	0.01
Sri Lanka	6,700	0.07
Singapore	3,100	0.15
Hong Kong	3,100	0.08
Republic of Korea	3,100	0.01

(Source: WHO/UNAIDS 1997)

What is even more alarming in India is that women are at a higher risk than men. A decade ago, women seemed to be on the periphery of the epidemic. In the 1980s, AIDS was primarily a male disease. Only 22% of women were affected. Today women comprise about 50% of infected cases. There are several reasons for this increase:

Biological reasons: Women are biologically more vulnerable than men to HIV infection. Studies show that male-to-female transmission of HIV is 2-4 times faster than female-to-male transmission.

Economic reasons: Many women have no choice. They are forced into commercial sex for reasons of economic survival. In India it is these women, who form the largest percentage of those carrying the AIDS virus.

Social reasons: Sexual subordination also leads to greater HIV vulnerability. Many men are sexually promiscuous. Their women often do not have the freedom to leave their spouses or to say "No" to their spouses. As a result, an increasing number of housewives in the metropolitan cities of India are being infected by these promiscuous partners, who have not taken the necessary precautions. Today this appears to be the standard route for infection of women.

A large part of the problem is **attitudinal**, based on monumental ignorance. One group of people believes that AIDS patients get what they deserve. This is a "Serve them right" attitude. This is not only petty but not based on facts. We can never be very sure of the origin of the disease. Many women, unknowingly and unwittingly, get AIDS from their lifelong spouse, who might have multiple sexual partners. Innocent children then get it from the mother! Many get it from blood transfusions. So, this attitude of "they had it coming" is inhumane to say the least.

Another attitude is one of indifference. "The problem does not affect me because I don't use drugs, I am not gay. I don't have multiple sexual partners. So I don't have to fear AIDS!" This attitude is foolish, because AIDS is not an **individual** problem. It is a **social** problem. The world in which we live is getting smaller and smaller and the problems of the community sooner or later affect each and every one of us.

The only proper attitude is a non-judgemental one. Once it is realized that most female AIDS victims contract the disease because they have no choice, the objective will be not to "correct their wicked behaviour" but to improve their choices and thus protect their **health** and **life.** This was the attitude of Jesus towards leprosy, the prevailing social stigma in the first century, which has a lot in common with AIDS today. It is the attitude of many religious sisters who have given up their regular work and have volunteered to serve with AIDS patients in community hospitals.

AIDS is not a problem that will go away. It is here to stay. We need to tackle it head on. Greater awareness and a change in attitudes is the first step in our strategy. Even simple contact with AIDS patients can be very illuminating. One religious sister narrates how a patient told her "From the moment I learned that I had AIDS, I really began to **live**. Before that I was dead. The reason: I began to see reality with the eye of compassion. I understood what it means to suffer!"

23
The Virgin Martyrs
Violence Against Women
❧

In the last decade we, in India, have been witness to
a series of incidents of violence against religious sisters,
some of which have ended in death. To name just a
few:

- o rape of two nuns at Gajraula in UP in 1990
- o murder of two nuns in Jogeshwari, Mumbai, 1990
- o 9 nuns molested in Amritsar, Punjab in 1992
- o 2 nuns assaulted in Punjab in 1993
- o murder of Sr Rani Maria of Udainagar in MP in 1995
- o 5 nuns brutally assaulted at Surya Nagar in UP in 1995
- o nun killed in Assam in 1995
- o gang-rape of 4 nuns at Jhabua in MP in 1998
- o nun beaten up, convent looted at Baghpat, UP in 1998
- o gang-rape of a woman working in a convent at Bandel, West Bengal

These are not stray cases. There is a pattern to this
violence. It may not be something calculated, but indirectly
it is a consequence of the work these sisters are doing,
viz. conscientizing and uplifting the poor and marginalized.
Somehow the work of these sisters threatens an
"insecure" political party that wants to keep the
marginalized down. The result is their violent reaction.

These sisters, whom I call, "martyrs" in the true sense
of the word, martyrs who died for their faith or martyrs

of survival—remind me very much of the virgin martyrs of early Christianity: Agatha, Agnes, Lucy, Cecilia, Anastasia and others. We are accustomed to think that these virgin martyrs died because they refused to get married to pagan Roman senators—that they preferred to die rather than lose their virginity. But the truth is far more complex. What has escaped us is the political nature of their death.

The Roman State needed a constant supply of young men to replenish their far flung legions in various parts of the empire. This led the Roman State to demand that young women marry and reproduce as a duty to the State. Thus, women who refused to marry were considered traitors and liable to be punished/killed. These Christian women martyrs refused to bow down to the State's definition of their life. They refused to reproduce children for the Roman army. They were "conscientious objectors" to the Roman Empire's programme of militaristic aggression. What they were saying in effect was: "We don't want to be part of your campaign of conquer and dominate!" and for this they were thrown to the wild beasts and became martyrs for the faith.[55]

There is a clear parallel between the virgin martyrs of early Christianity and the religious sisters of North India who were raped, assaulted or murdered. The sisters were all working for the poor—for tribals, for Adivasis, for Harijans. In various ways, they enabled these voiceless people to get conscientized, to organize themselves, to have the courage to address their own problems. Sr Rani Maria, in particular, by her work directly challenged the Panchayat leader. The efforts of others like the sisters of Jhabua, were less direct, but equally, they too were seen in some way as a threat to the powers that be.

We notice a close association between state militarism and violence against women, just as there is a close association between a fundamentalist agenda and repression of minorities. Now we can understand the statement of the Vishwa Hindu Parishad justifying the gang-rape of the four nuns at Jhabua in MP. The VHP described it as the result of the 'anger of patriotic Hindu youth against conversions'. As if to say patriotism can ever justify gang-rape or uplifting the poor can ever be labelled 'conversion work'. All of this only serves to bring out the terrible insecurity of the VHP and the Sangh Parivar whenever they find anyone defending the rights of the poor and oppressed. All of this is telling us that martyrdom is being re-enacted... the story of Christ is being retold.

24
Women are not for Burning
೨

In the last few years we have witnessed shocking atrocities perpetrated on women. Most of these go unreported. Here however are a few examples from those that have been reported.

- Shirin Juwaley, a young girl, realized from the very first day of her marriage, that it was a disaster. Finding it impossible to live with her husband, she returned to her widowed mother and asked her husband for a divorce. He refused saying that he wanted a lakh of rupees first. Since she could not afford it, Shirin decided to forget the divorce and live as a single woman with her mother. While walking on the street one day, her husband appeared out of nowhere and flung acid on her face. It was only when she saw the emanating fumes that Shirin realized what had happened. Shirin suffered third degree burns. Though both her eyes were spared, her face was completely disfigured. Meanwhile, that very night, her husband took a flight to Kuwait and till today is absconding.

- Aparna Prabhu, a pretty 20-year-old girl living in the city of Mumbai, was harassed from her school days by a boy staying opposite her building. She had always ignored him even though she was afraid of him. One day he proposed marriage to her. When Aparna walked away without giving an answer, the boy crept up from behind and poured acid on her. She was rushed to the hospital, but lost her eye and the rest of her body was badly scarred. The boy was caught, but within 4 months had been let out on bail. So, while the boy is roaming the streets freely, Aparna continues to suffer, staring deformity in the face, and has to undergo painful treatment and repeated surgery.[56]

- A priest was asked to come and bless the dead body of a young woman, mother of two children. They said it was a case of accidental burning. The woman was cooking and her sari caught fire. Not satisfied with the answer, the priest asked a few questions from the neighbours. They told him that the young woman was often seen crying bitterly. At times they heard her screams. The priest, very sensibly, refused to perform the burial without a post-mortem, even though the father-in-law and mother-in-law kept pressing him to finish the ceremony. Later investigations revealed that the young woman was being harassed for dowry and it was the in-laws themselves who had poured kerosene over her and consigned her to the flames.

Why do these things happen? And why only to women? Above all, why only to young women between the ages of 18 to 24. No doubt statistics tell us that one out of three persons, who suffer from burn accidents, are from India. Yes, but all these are not accidents. Most of them are deliberate acts of violence or revenge that occur mostly within the context of family and relationships. It is as though these men feel that since they cannot have the women for themselves, they want to make sure that nobody else can have them.

It is ironic that fire, which was stolen by Prometheus from the heavens, for the benefit of humanity, is now being used to disfigure, destroy and consign women to a life of hell-fire here on earth itself.

All this points to certain attitudes and perceptions in our society that still needs to be changed. One is the perception of the **male ownership of women** reflected in statements such as: "If I can't have you, nobody else will!" Or worse, "If I ask you for something, you, as a woman, have *no right* to say no!" A second equally widespread and accepted attitude is the **male dominance over wealth and decision-making.** As long as men continue to hold the purse strings of the household and make all the major decisions in the family, any woman who has dared to question, complain or resist such dominance has felt the resounding thud of a man's slap, a kick in the abdomen or worse still the pain and impact of a physical instrument. And this not just once or twice but repeatedly. A third related attitude is the **acceptance of violence as a means to settle interpersonal disputes.** One observes this even on the streets, when even a slight traffic accident ends up in blows and a physical free-for-all. People get out of their cars, rickshaws, roll up their sleeves and begin banging away with their fists. As though this is the only way to settle such matters. As long as this culture persists—with its mindset that violence is the only way to settle problems—women will continue to be battered because of their inferior physical skills. Finally, the last prevailing attitude is **a concept of masculinity that is synonymous with toughness, male honour or dominance.** Quite often people have the mistaken notion that to be masculine means to be tough, physical and aggressive, while to be feminine means to be passive, soft and resilient. This is not only a false idea of masculinity but is a perspective that is the root cause of all aggressiveness, wars and the building up of military power.

All religions respect fire. It is considered a symbol of divine energy and is used in many religious ceremonies. But when fire is used to punish or destroy other human beings, not only are we degrading our fellow human beings, but worse still, we are unduly usurping for ourselves divine prerogatives—and lo and behold—the consequences of such actions will be disastrous not just for the entire human race but for the entire cosmos.

25
Sexual Harassment at the Workplace
❧

Case one: Lata is a clerk in the railways. Her supervisor purposely blocks the door every time she tries to go out. He has often tried to pin her against the doorway asking her why she is in such a hurry and to make some time for him too. He has hinted that her acceptance will ensure an easy passage to promotion. Lata has consistently refused to entertain his advances. For the last 10 years now, she has received no promotion, either in salary or status and is unable to advance professionally.

Case two: When Sunita, who works as a government servant in the PWD department, complained about the corruption of a senior government official, she began to face all forms of crude treatment from her colleagues, who resented her reporting the case. Posters of nude women, with Sunita's face superimposed on them, were pinned on the wall in front of her desk. Often, when official memos were passed around, lewd scribbles, referring to Sunita as a loose woman, would be added on. She constantly received anonymous calls, some of them obscene and some of them open invitations to spend the night out. Sometimes when she walked across to the washroom, sexually offensive comments were made pertaining to her appearance.

Are both these cases instances of sexual harassment at work? Yes, definitely!!! Both Lata and Sunita are certainly victims. Lata's is a case of '**quid pro**

quo' harassment, when a person in authority, usually a supervisor, demands sexual favours from a subordinate as a condition of a job benefit. In the second case, Sunita is not threatened with job termination or lack of advancement; however, she suffers repeated abuse from **a hostile work environment**. Her co-workers, engaging in unwelcome and inappropriate sexually based behaviour, render the work-atmosphere intimidating, hostile, or offensive, and in the process are grossly violating her rights.

On August 13, 1997, in the famous case of Vishaka and others versus the State of Rajasthan, a landmark decision by the Supreme Court defined the framework of sexual harassment at the workplace. Sexual harassment was defined as:

- Physical contact and advances
- Demand or request for sexual favours
- Sexually coloured remarks or propositions
- Display of pornography
- Any other unwelcome verbal or non-verbal conduct of sexual nature.

In spite of the fact that there is a proposed bill in the Lok Sabha to curb sexual harassment and violence against women, there are still a lot of misconceptions and myths in the minds and attitudes of most people in our country. Here is a sample:

Myth no. 1: *Sexual harassment at the work place is an isolated western phenomenon. It happens very seldom in India.*

Answer: Not true at all!! According to a 1997 study conducted by **Sakshi**, New Delhi, between **40 to 60 percent of working women** experienced some form of sexual harassment at the workplace.

Myth no. 2: *Sexual harassment is a middle class, urban phenomenon, experienced mainly by women who work in* *offices. Women, who are bold, outspoken and who wear revealing westernized clothes, are most likely to be harassed.*

Answer: Again, not at all true!! According to studies reported by the ILO (International Labour Organization, New Delhi) a large number of victims are the family planning workers, gram sevikas, nurses, midwives and social workers in the rural areas. The crucial factor seems to be the relatively low status of women in work sectors. So, whether in an urban or rural setting, if sexual harassment stems from a woman's inferior position in the job, it also functions as a peg that holds women there.

Myth no. 3: *Sexual harassment is normal behaviour and a woman should feel complimented by it.*

Answer: Sexual harassment is about power. It is a tactic to dominate by embarrassment or degradation. It is not an expression of healthy human relationships.

Myth no. 4: *Even if I am harassed at the workplace, there is nothing I can do about it!!*

Answer: There is something you can do!! At a first level, you can raise the issue with the complaints committee of your organization, which has then to investigate the issue. There is an obligation on employers to set into motion a complaints committee such that at least 50 percent of the persons in it are female. If the management fails to do this, the next option available is to file a criminal case against the employer. After all, it is the employer's responsibility to see that a safe working environment exists.

A young woman, applying for a secretarial position in a prestigious pharmaceutical company, had completed all her interviews successfully and now had to pass the final hurdle, the medical test. The interviewing doctor insisted that he had to feel her breasts in order to pass the test. 'If you refuse', he

94

said, 'I will fail you. You cannot complain because you are not yet an employee!' She refused and did not pass the test. Later she found that several other young prospective applicants had had a similar experience with the same doctor. She managed to get 6 of them together and they signed a common letter of protest to the company. The company initiated a complaints committee and the doctor was dismissed. Four of the six girls subsequently got good positions in the company and are currently working there.

In conclusion, it must be stressed that in most sexual harassment cases it is the men who harass the women. This leads us to become aware of the social values and mores perpetuated by our society. If attitudes and mind-sets are so important, then schools and colleges are the seedbed or training ground for sexual harassment. These institutions must have special programmes or courses to initiate young men and women into the dynamics of what constitutes sexual harassment, what its root cause is and how to deal with it. Only then can a woman begin to experience freedom and equality at the workplace.

26
Family Law
Reprieve for Women?

=========== ❦ ===========

Marriage and Family, we say, are pillar institutions in society. Yet, for over 100 years, Christians were unconcerned that their statutes on marriage and the family were unchanged. The government has now moved to bring about changes with new Amendments, so as to bring about greater parity between men and women, but there is still a long way to go. This essay will treat only of two changes—in the Guardianship Act and Divorce Act.

Guardianship of the Child

As part of my work in the Marriage Tribunal I prepare petitions for the dissolution of Christian marriages in which there has been no proper consent. Recently one of the petitions was granted a hearing and the marriage was annulled. Subsequently the couple got divorced. There remains however the sad problem of guardianship of the child. The child is 10-years-old and the mother is terribly afraid that guardianship (rights to decide about the child) will probably be given to the father. This, despite the fact that she has looked after the child during the period of separation, and also despite the fact that she and her divorced spouse have professional jobs and salaries of similar ranking. Since both are Christians they fall under the Guardian and Wards Act of 1890. According to this really ancient piece of legislation, section 19, the father is normally given priority in the matter of guardianship unless there is clear evidence to prove that he is unfit.

For Hindus, however, there is a more recent but equally discriminatory piece of legislation called the Hindu Minority and Guardianship Act of 1956. In mid-February 1999 the interpretation of this Act was challenged in the Courts. The case goes back to 1995, when Gita Hariharan had gone to open a Bank Account with the Reserve Bank of India in the name of her child Rishab. She was told quite bluntly "You are not the natural guardian of the child. Your husband is!" Gita Hariharan moved the courts and in February 1999, Judge Bannerjee issued a landmark decision stating: "Gender equality is one of the basic features of our constitution. Disqualification of a mother to act as a guardian *during the lifetime of the father* would definitely run counter to the constitutional mandate and would lead to a differentiation between male and female. The father by reason of a dominant personality cannot be ascribed to have a preferential right over the mother in the matter of guardianship since both fall within the same category." In other words, the Hindu mother can now be considered guardian **even during the lifetime of the father**. Gradually, there is a move towards giving both mother and father equal rights for either to become the guardian of a child.

This decision at present holds only for Hindus under the Hindu Minority and Guardianship Act. It is now up to others—Christians, Parsis and others—to move the courts regarding their own situation so that the ruling becomes universal. Muslims, of course, have their own personal Law, but here too, the father is the natural guardian.

The criterion to decide guardianship of children was always a problem even in Biblical times. A beautiful story is told in the Bible (1 Kings 3:16-28) about the wisdom of Solomon. Two Hebrew women, both innkeepers, were

97

fighting over the rights to a child. Originally, they both had infants, but one of them lost her child. Now, both were making competing claims about the surviving child. Each claimed it to be her own. There were no witnesses and King Solomon had to decide to whom he should award guardianship. Solomon used guile. He sent for a sword and when it was brought, he said: "Cut the living child into two and give each woman half of it!" The real mother, her heart full of love for her son, said to the king, "Please, Your Majesty, don't kill the child. Give it to her!" But the other woman said, "Don't give it to either of us. Go ahead and cut it into two." Then Solomon said, "Don't kill the child. Give it to the first woman— she is its real mother!"

King Solomon's wise principle was that love for the child is the only true criterion for deciding who should look after the child. I think all of us (the Courts included) can take a leaf out of the judgement of Solomon. It is so anachronistic to see the Courts giving guardianship of the child to the father, even though he is an alcoholic, even though he has never shown any interest in the child—but just because he is the higher earning member and just because he is male. In this sense, Judge Bannerjee's decision which states that *both parents ought to be treated as guardians of the minor,* is a progressive step for women's equality and growth of the child. Reform of the law and the development of a universal code of guardianship is an essential objective for those interested in the welfare of the woman/mother and her child.

Divorce for Christians

For more than a century, now Christians have lived under the Indian Christian Marriage Act of 1872 and the Indian Divorce Act of 1869. Both these acts were drawn up mainly for British residents in India at a time when the circumstances of marriage were quite different.

Since then things have changed rapidly and these acts have become obsolete. Hence, it is very clear that there is need for a change in the law. The Indian Divorce Act of 1869 is a typical example. For instance, under this act, Christian men could apply for divorce on grounds of simple adultery (even a single act would suffice), whereas Christian women had to prove prolonged or aggravated adultery or adultery with additional grounds of cruelty or desertion. Now, under the new amendment to the Act the grounds will be made equal for men and women. Further, there is also the additional option of divorce by mutual consent. If this comes through, it will be a significant reprieve for women who have been suffering under the unequal terms of the previous Act. The second change refers to sections 17 and 20. Earlier the decree of divorce pronounced by the District Court had to be confirmed by the High Court within a period of 6 months. These six months meant additional harassment and tension for the woman, especially if the trial itself had already taken a toll of her energies. Under the new amendment, the District Court's verdict will be final and there will be no need of further confirmation.[57] If these amendments are passed, life for many women will be a veritable "release", governed as they presently are, by antiquated laws.

Epilogue:

The Amendments to the Indian Divorce Act were passed by Parliament in August 2001 and have been welcomed by women and by members of the minority community. However lots more remains to be done. There are still other pending demands, namely amendment to the Indian Succession Act of 1925 and also enactment of a Christian Adoption Act.[58] Only then will women in the Christian community be treated at par with men. Unfortunately, in our country, most bills and laws concerning women are coursing along on a slow track. The best way for a bill to become law is through informed public opinion. As Wendell Phillips said more than a century ago "The law is nothing unless close behind it stands a warm, living, public opinion". If we want Christian Marriage and Family laws that are really effective and helpful, then we must make ourselves aware of the antiquated laws, discuss, critique and express our opinions, have a public debate, and thus facilitate the process by which the law really becomes the 'will of the people'.

III

Her Stories

27
Is Compassion a Feminine Quality?
Mother Teresa
ଏ

In the second week of September 1997 we witnessed the magnificent funeral ceremonies of two famous women, both public figures, both gifted with an extraordinary charism for compassionate work—Mother Teresa and Princess Diana. I fell to thinking about this quality of compassion. Three questions arose in my mind:

1) *Is compassion a typically feminine quality?*

When one considers the large number of women who go in for professions like nursing, social work, care of the aged, counselling and teaching children, it appears to be true. However, I don't believe that compassion is *biologically* given to women. Rather, it appears to be *culturally* acquired. In the inculcation of values in childhood some qualities are given greater prominence than others. And in most women, qualities of the heart are stressed much more than in men. Yet each woman allows these stirrings of her heart to affect her to different degrees and intensity.

Diana was given to compassionate work, probably because of the sufferings she experienced in her own life. Mother Teresa, during the 20 years she was a Loreto nun in India, felt searingly the sufferings of the destitute. In the year 1946 in Calcutta, as she looked out of her convent room, she was greeted by a horrifying image. There, in the slums next door, was a man sleeping on the ground and being bitten by a rat. The man had no strength to pull himself up and run away from the rat. He just lay there and allowed himself to be eaten away. That ghastly vision was a turning point in her life. She left the Loreto convent and founded her own Missionaries of Charity, an order that was expressly founded to look after the unwanted, the dying, the destitute, the poorest of the poor.

2) *How does one generate compassion or karuna?*

This question was often asked of Mother Teresa: "How do you maintain such a high level of energy and such untiring compassion?" Her answer was as quick as it was simple: "My faith and my religious motivation." No ordinary social worker, no matter how dedicated, could have faced the daily horrors she did, without succumbing to depression. Mother Teresa used her relationship to God as a fulcrum to tackle the mundane, in much the same way as a workman makes use of a lever to lift a load which would otherwise prove too heavy to bear. A rich businessman once asked her: "How is it that you are able to do such repugnant tasks? Even if somebody gave me a lakh of rupees I would not do such tasks!" Pat came her reply, "Neither would I—purely for a lakh of rupees!"

3) *Isn't compassionate work only a partial answer to the problem of poverty and suffering?*

This is one of the biggest criticisms levelled against Mother Teresa and her work. Her answer however was sure and emphatic. "It is partial no doubt, but it is essential! Of what use are medicine and efficiency without love! Each one must make his or her own limited contribution. If others are working for more radical solutions, so much the better. My task is to offer to the poorest a chance to live and die in dignity!" And this she did exceedingly well.

When the journalist Jug Suraiya visited 'Nirmal Hriday', home for the dying destitute in Kalighat, Calcutta, he expected to be greeted by the powerful stench of death, he imagined that people would be crying out with pain, he envisioned bodies of the sick with open sores oozing out pus, but when he actually entered the home, he was struck by the peace and quiet of the place. The inmates lay on pallets on the clean-swept floor of a large, airy room. Sisters in white sarees were walking about efficiently attending to patients and there prevailed an atmosphere of serenity and tranquility. Just then a skeleton of a man was brought in. "He was brought to us too late", Mother Teresa said softly as she bent over to examine him. "Even though he could not live in dignity, we shall offer him a place to die in dignity!"[59]

Today, all over the world, Mother Teresa has left a legacy of 540 houses where the poorest of the poor are given a shelter. This may not solve the problems of the world, but who can deny that they definitely improve the quality of the lives of the poor. No wonder that during her life she received every award on the face of this earth. The President of India, in his short eulogy on the death of Mother Teresa, said: "Such a woman as her but rarely walks this earth!"

28
Christian in Faith, Hindu in Lifestyle
Pandita Ramabai: Social Reformer
ᘓ

Is it possible to be Hindu and Christian at the same time? Apparently yes, if one understands Hinduism like Pandita Ramabai, not as a religion, but as a *way of life*. She integrated in her person the beliefs of Christianity with the lifestyle of Hinduism and became one of the great social reformers of modern India. Unfortunately, her contribution to women's emancipation has been eclipsed by the storm of controversy over her evangelizing work, but more and more she is being recognized for the great foundations she laid in the field of women's empowerment.

Born in 1858, a Chitpavan Brahmin from Maharashtra, she was a Sanskrit scholar, well versed in the Vedas. At the young age of twenty she was given the titles of 'Pandita' and 'Saraswati'. However, Ramabai was disillusioned with the restrictive norms laid down for women in the Hindu law codes. According to the Hindu Shastras woman could only attain Moksha by worshipping her husband *as a god*. If her husband died, the young widow was encouraged to immolate herself on the funeral pyre and then perhaps in her next life she could be born again as a man.

On the other hand, Ramabai was edified by the work of the Christian (Anglican) sisters. In her *Testimony*, she says, "I asked the sisters to tell me what it was that made the Christians care for and reclaim the commercial sex workers. I had never heard or seen anything of the kind done for this class of women by Hindus in my own country!"[60] Ramabai gradually read the story of Christ, his conversation with the Samaritan woman, became attracted to the gospel of Luke, and soon was baptized.

Although she questioned the way of salvation proposed by the Hindu Scriptures, she remained faithful to Hindu ways and to Hindu tradition. A vegetarian all her life, she even did without garlic and onions, and remained committed to the practice of fasting. Her biographer, D.N. Tilak claims that she did not cease being a Hindu in her culture.[61] She was the first to advocate strongly that Hindi and not English should become the link language in India. Her homes and schools were run along Hindu lines, even though she permitted conversions to Christianity, without advocating them. No wonder that Sarojini Naidu, at the Memorial service in honour of Pandita Ramabai, said: "She is the first Christian in the calendar of Hindu saints."[62]

It is this Hindu-Christian identity that, far from hindering her work, spurred her to give an impetus to the cause of women in India. She founded the Arya Mahila Samaj and was one of the first *women* to be a *member* of the Indian National Congress. In the Social Conference in 1889 she moved a resolution which condemned the custom of disfiguring child widows by cutting their hair and keeping their heads shaven. In 1897, during the famous plague, she protested so strongly against the treatment given to women in the public hospitals that her protests even found an echo in the British Parliament. Her life-long work however consisted in the establishment of homes, training centres and trade schools for women; Sharda Sadan (for child widows),

Kripa Sadan (for sex workers) and Mukti Sadan (for poor and starving women and children).

For those of us who are groping to find a way of living out our Indian Christianity, Pandita Ramabai has shown us a path. Christian in her beliefs, she was Hindu in her way of life. Her universal love was expressed in her work for women and women's rights, in her striving for reform. Side by side with her work of running her homes, she single-handedly translated the entire Bible into Marathi. In his autobiography Maharshi Dondo Karve, referring to Ramabai, writes: "Women of her calibre at any time, not only in India, but in the whole world, can be counted on your five fingers!"[63]

29
Brave Fighter for Democracy and Justice
Aung San Suu Kyi
cؗ

Aung San Suu Kyi is an extraordinary woman, perhaps the world's most famous political dissident; in the words of Vaclav Havel, "one of the most outstanding examples of the power of the powerless". A slightly built woman, not more than 100 lbs, who often wears a flower in her hair, Aung San Suu Kyi may be as delicate as a butterfly but has a backbone of steel.

The daughter of Aung San, national hero and founder of independent Burma, she was only two when her father was assassinated. Growing up in India, where her mother was appointed ambassador, she went on to Oxford to study politics, philosophy and economics. In 1972 she married Michael Aris, an Oxford professor of Tibetan Buddhism and with their two sons, Alexander and Kim, the couple lived a quiet academic life until 1988.

Things took a dramatic turn when she returned to Burma (now Myanmar) to nurse her ailing mother. At the time the country was under military dictatorship and in political turmoil. Soldiers had opened fire on 3000 peaceful demonstrators. Aung San Suu Kyi decided "that as her father's daughter she could not remain indifferent to all that was happening" and so, in 1988, before 500,000 people, in front of Shwedegon Pagoda in

Rangoon (now Yangon), she announced her momentous decision to enter the political struggle for democracy.

Quickly assuming leadership of NLD (National League for Democracy) her vigorous campaigning for the general elections resulted in a landslide victory, her party winning 392 out of 485 seats. However, the SLORC, the new military command, simply refused to honour her victory, placed her under arrest and kept her in political isolation, a "prisoner in her own home and country".

Aung San Suu Kyi however continued to speak out boldly and courageously (often through tapes that were smuggled outside the country) at times calming her supporters when they wanted to get violent. It was during this period of confinement and house arrest that she was awarded the Nobel Prize for Peace in 1991.

Sacrifice

The military junta told her that if she left the country to accept the award, they would not allow her to return. And so Aung San Suu Kyi made the difficult decision to stay behind in Myanmar, and support her people's struggle for democracy, giving up both the honour of accepting the Nobel Prize and the physical closeness with her family in England. From her house in Yangon however she was allowed to hold public meetings and thousands came to listen to her weekly speeches.

The "lady in chains" now became world-renowned and the military leadership, afraid of international sanctions, released her from house arrest in 1995. Nonetheless, not very much changed for Aung San Suu Kyi. Her movements continued to be restricted for several years and only very recently was there a slight relaxation of the strict surveillance accorded her.

The year 1998 would ask one more sacrifice of Aung San Suu Kyi. Her husband Michael was diagnosed with terminal cancer. Again, the military junta told her that if she left to be by his side, she would not be allowed into the country again. She had to make the agonizing decision of choosing between her "ailing" husband and her "suffering" people. She chose again to be with her people, while her husband succumbed to cancer.

Non-violence

What makes this courageous woman unique is her commitment to non-violence, both *as a principle* and *as a tactic*. Unlike Mandela, for her there is no exception to non-violence. Unlike Gandhi, she does not condemn those who are violent. Her "revolution of the spirit" is best explained in her famous essay "Freedom from Fear".[64] Even though physically attacked and terrorized several times, she remains unafraid for herself. "The only fear I have is *fear for my people*", she says. In 1989 while walking with a group of supporters, a squad of soldiers jumped out of their vehicle and took aim at Aung San Suu Kyi and her friends. Motioning to the others to scatter, she walked up to the soldiers and stood directly in front of their raised rifles. "It seemed so much simpler to provide them with a single target than to bring everyone else in," she explained. The soldiers retreated.

Economics

Aung San Suu Kyi believes that politics cannot be separated from economics. Her strategy to pressure the military dictatorship consists of her famous appeal to governments and multi-nationals to disinvest from Myanmar and "take your investments elsewhere please". This has earned her a few critics and hostility from her own government. She continues however to speak out fearlessly emphasizing that multi-national investments in Myanmar are only making the few rich richer. "In some ways it is better," she says, "to have the people of the world on your side than the governments or corporations of the world."

Epilogue

The struggle goes on. Democracy has not come to Myanmar. Aung San Suu Kyi continues to hold out a candle of hope to her people. In the words of her son, quoting from the Hindu Vedas, at the funeral of his father:

"For yesterday is but a dream
And tomorrow is only a vision.
But today well-lived
makes every yesterday a dream of happiness
And every tomorrow a vision of hope.
Look well therefore to this day."

30
Women of Courage
Diana Ortiz and Taslima Nasreen
~c~

Diana Ortiz is an Ursuline American sister, who was working with the Mayans in the highlands of Guatemala. One night, in 1989, she was picked up by a group of Contra forces and gang-raped. While this brutal molestation of her body was going on, one of the senior officers in the Contra forces entered the room and shouted at the soldiers "Stop it! What are you doing? Don't you realize that this woman is different. She is Americana! A religious sister! She can get us into trouble!"

Then he whisked Diana off into a jeep (apparently with the purpose of convincing her to be silent) but Diana managed to leap out from the jeep while it stood waiting at a traffic light. Disappearing into the crowds, she managed to telephone her convent and from there found her way back clandestinely into the U.S.

It was then that her second struggle began. She tried to dig up information and find out the real reason as to why she was picked up and gang-raped. Was her kidnapping and abduction a simple case of mistaken identity or was it because she was part of the liberation movement? Was it a simple case of being in the wrong place at the wrong time, or was there a deliberate effort by the Contra forces to thwart the liberation movement? She knew that the US government backed the Contra forces, but was there some complicity on the part of the US government in her kidnapping and abduction? That was the real objective of her search. She had good leads, but each time she came up against the blank wall of *'classified information'*. She paid several visits to the White House to try to get to the bottom of this vast cover-up. She even got a personal assurance from Mrs. Clinton that she would do all in her power to get the relevant information declassified. But till today, over 10 years later, she is at an impasse in her investigation.[65] But Diana has not given up. Her fight still goes on. She would like to uncover the truth not just for herself, but for the hundreds of other men and women, who were killed or raped by Contra forces.

The Story of Taslima Nasreen

The second woman of courage is a doctor turned journalist, Taslima Nasreen, forced to live in exile because she defied the fundamentalist ideas of the religious leaders of her country, Bangladesh. Taslima wrote a book documenting the hardships and persecution of a neighbouring *Hindu family* in a Muslim dominated area of Bangladesh, in the wake of the communal riots that followed the Babri Masjid demolition in India. For this, the Muslim leaders pronounced three 'fatwas' or denunciations against her.

Not to be outdone, the spirited Taslima wrote an article suggesting that the Shariat law be changed because it discriminated against women. Responding to her letter, a columnist accused Taslima for being anti-Muslim because she wanted the "Koran" to be changed. Taslima immediately wrote back saying that she could never have asked for the Koran to be changed for the simple reason that she didn't believe in the Koran. What she had asked for was a change in Shariat law, and there was a difference between the Koran and the Shariat. By now, all the fundamentalist religious leaders were up in arms against her and she was advised by her friends to leave the country secretly. Taslima now lives abroad but continues through her writing, especially through her books, to speak out for all women and oppressed.

113

A Reflection on their Stories

What do we see in common between these two women? There is no doubt about their **fearlessness** despite hardships and persecution in their pursuit of truth. Both women have taken on the awesome might of powerful fundamentalist forces and courageously continue to fight despite severe consequences to their lives.

But there is something else also in common. Both women began from personal, individual problems and moved to larger, societal problems. Diana began with her own rape, but now is struggling to uncover the truth for hundreds of others who suffered at the hands of the Contra forces. Taslima began by reporting on her immediate neighbour's story of persecution, by defending her journalistic account, but now has become the voice for all women and all oppressed peoples, not only of Bangladesh, but of the entire world, who suffer discrimination on account of religion or politics.

In the Old Testament we have the story of Hannah, who went through a similar movement from personal to public issues. She began by praying to Yahweh to put an end to her barrenness, because she had become the ridicule of all. However, when God answered her prayer, Hannah became concerned about all those who experienced similar rejection. Her second prayer (I Sam 2) praising God "for raising the lowly from the dust and giving them a place among the great" became the model for the famous Magnificat of Mary.

31
Modern Woman Prophet Of India
Medha Patkar
ೞ

In the second book of Samuel, chapter 21, we read the story of Rizpah, who was a concubine of King Saul. Rizpah had two sons but after Saul had died, a group of Gibeonites approached David and complained that Saul had tried to wipe them out. In recompense, they wanted the death of seven of Saul's offspring. David handed over seven of Saul's sons, two of whom happened to be Armoni and Mephibosheth, sons of Rizpah. The Gibeonites executed these men on the mountain and left their corpses there to rot. It was then that Rizpah made her protest, her famous 'dharna'. She went up to the mountain and kept vigil over the corpses. Sheltering herself with sackcloth, she sat there all alone day and night, from spring until autumn, protecting the corpses from the birds and wild animals. When David came to hear of this, he took heed immediately and ordered a solemn and decent burial for the seven men. Rizpah's action can be considered 'prophetic'. Her lonely 'dharna' on the mountain was to some extent successful in that it drew the attention of King David and claimed justice for her sons.

A prophet in the Biblical sense is not one who foretells the future, but one who interprets God's will. It is for this reason that a prophet denounces any kind of *injustice*, because injustice is against the divine will.[66] A second characteristic about prophetic action is that in calling attention to the cause of the victim, the method used is always *non-violent*.

Medha Patkar can be considered a modern woman prophet. A quiet, unobtrusive social worker, she took up the cause of the rehabilitation of tribals displaced by the Sardar Sarovar Dam. The dam submerges more than 37,000 hectares of forest and agricultural land and displaces about 3,20,000 villagers whose livelihood depends on these natural resources. If resettled at all, the tribals have been placed on arid, uncultivable land.[67] The uniqueness of Medha's protests is that they have always been non-violent. Over the last 15 years, under the organization called NBA (Narmada Bachao Andolan), she has mobilized massive protest rallies, hunger fasts, village to village padayatras, gheraos, blockades and marches. The NBA's most original method has been 'jal samarpan', a method of resistance by which villagers cling to their homes even at the cost of being submerged.[68] Medha herself stood for hours in chest deep water until the submergence 'order' had been called off. She almost died in a 22-day hunger strike in 1991. Her efforts have been partly successful. The World Bank withdrew its funds after an independent review and reassessment of the entire project. However, the state governments of Gujarat, Maharashtra and Madhya Pradesh have vowed to carry on with the venture and recently the Supreme Court permitted the dam to be raised to a height of 90 metres.

The struggle however goes on. Medha will not give up. She has spent half her life for the NBA and literally become grey in the process. She has now founded a National Alliance of People's Movements, which works at a broader level and seeks to question the government's concept of development and its repercussions on the environment. On the constructive side, the NAPM has initiated alternatives to energy, water harvesting and education for tribal children.

Once, when she addressed a gathering of priests, sisters and seminarians, she narrated her problems with the police—how she literally had to run from them, go underground, hide in villages, travel by night and stay without food for days on end. One of the sisters then asked her "How are you able to bear all these sufferings?" and Medha answered "I honestly don't think of them as 'sufferings'. My goal is to help the tribals and villagers. In the process one has to undergo some hardships. You might call them sufferings but I look upon them as 'a means to a cause'!" In these words, she described her simple faith in justice.

Medha has received numerous awards, national and international: the Deena Nath Mangeshkar Award, the Mahatma Phule Award, the Right to Livelihood Award, the Goldman Environment Prize, the Green Ribbon Award for Best International Political Campaigner from the BBC and the Human Rights Defender's Award from Amnesty International.

What remains outstanding is her undaunted and unflinching spirit. Like Rizpah, in the book of Samuel, she has not been deterred by physical hunger, the blistering cold or wild animals. Nothing but the cause of the voiceless, powerless people has kept her going.

IV

Towards Feminization of the Church

32
Paradigms for Feminization
of the Church
❦

The word 'feminist' often has a bad connotation.
Many feel that feminists are aggressive, that they
delight in 'male-bashing', and are somewhat
intimidating and threatening. This has prevented many
from wanting to study feminist theology. Nevertheless this
is not the real meaning of the word feminist. The word
feminist means 'egalitarian' or 'mutually respectful'. By
"feminization of the Church" is not meant a Church, which
puts on a "feminine" face or a Church which puts on
feminine characteristics, (just as for 2000 years we had
a masculine or male-dominated Church); by feminization
is meant not only a Church that has shed its patriarchal
characteristics, or a Church that sees the increasing and
visible presence of women in it, but most importantly, by
feminization is meant a Church that *treats everyone
equally, that is mutually respectful, that has a cosmopolitan,
cross cultural consciousness.* To understand this position, we
need therefore to look at some of the paradigms or models
that feminists operate from.[69] I can visualize four paradigms:

The 'sameness' paradigm: According to this paradigm,
women demand equal rights or the same rights that men
have previously appropriated. Thus, if previously, men
were allowed to vote, women should now be allowed to
vote. If men have a football team, women too should
have the right to have a football team. If men have a

9. Dare to see...

right to ordination, women should also be allowed the right to ordination. In this paradigm women want the 'same' things that men are allowed. This model does not sufficiently recognize the fact that women are different from men both biologically and culturally.

The complementary paradigm: According to this paradigm, women are no longer the fairer sex, the weaker sex, but the complementary sex. The sexes complete each other. While, in theory, this sounds fine, in practice it means that women have to complement the tasks that men have already decided for themselves. Men are supposed to be, by nature, active, rational, adventurous and assertive; women are supposed to be passive, caring, compassionate and emotional. Men are to go out and work, be the breadwinners; while women are supposed to stay at home and look after the children and the household. Theoretically, this model is fine, but in practice it turns out that men decide the model and the roles in this model. Women are simply supposed to complement the role of men.

The sisterhood paradigm: According to this thinking, women as a group must stick together and form their own sisterhood. Such women have spoken in terms of leaving the male-dominated church and forming their own church with separate services, with a separate women's Bible and a separate lectionary. Women, they feel, need to have an exodus from the male-dominated Church in order to experience their liberation. This model not only emphasizes the differences between men and women, but also insists on different and separate structures for men and for women.

The solidarity paradigm: This is a paradigm that arises typically in Asian cultures. According to this model, the issues of peasants, workers, dalits, tribals and ecology are all connected. There is an interface and interaction between sexism, racism, casteism, colonialism, militarism, fundamentalism and environmental destruction. Patriarchy is not just about males dominating females but is *any kind of* subordination and domination. Thus women must collaborate/network with other oppressed groups like workers, tribals and dalits. The issues of all these groups are interlinked. Violence, for instance, whether domestic or public (like in communal riots) must be analyzed in all its interlinkages. Feminism, according to this approach, is a *way of thinking* that develops connections between social forces. This is the model that would seem most appropriate for women in third world countries.

Which kind of paradigm did the Jesus movement espouse? According to St. Luke, even though Jesus did not use the words, Jesus seemed to follow the solidarity paradigm. Jesus mixed and mingled with the oppressed peoples of society: women, widows, tax collectors, prostitutes, lepers, the physically handicapped, sinners, farmers and fishermen. He had dinner with them, he went around with them, he announced to them the 'good news'—the hope that one day there would be a new age when 'the last shall be first, the hungry will be filled, and the lowly will be exalted'. The Jesus movement became a solidarity of slaves, Gentiles, tax collectors, women and outcasts of society. The symbol of their solidarity was the Eucharist.

Feminist groups that do not want to join hands with other oppressed groups either become isolated or tend to diminish in numbers.

33
Women Office Holders in Early Church
≈ ≈

At a parish council meeting, a councillor raised the question, "Why are our masses and liturgical services attended mostly by women? Could it be that women come to church to meet certain emotional needs?" "If that were so," parried one of the women, "how does one explain that all over the world most parish organizations and church social work activities are staffed and operated by women? Instead of *women needing the Church*, it seems to me, that *the Church needs women!*" To this the councillor had no answer.

Yes, it is a fact, that not only in modern times, but from the very beginnings of Church history, women have been very active in the Christian community. Unfortunately, writings about women in the Bible have often referred to them as mothers, sisters, daughters, wives and hetaerae; in other words, reduced them to their biological functions. That is why, it is heartening to read some of the latest research which describes women as holding important offices in the early Christian communities: apostle, prophet, deacon, teacher, hostess of the household church, missionary co-worker and ministry of the 'widow'.

Apostle: One of the women apostles in the early church was **Junia**, who along with her partner Andronicus, were referred to by Paul as "outstanding apostles".[70] Both of them were Christians before Paul and suffered in prison with him (Romans 16:7). No doubt the term 'apostle' had very different meanings in the early church.[71] In its broadest sense, even Mary Magdalene and the other women at the tomb, as well as the Samaritan woman in Jn 4, have been referred to as "apostles".

Prophet: A second charism held by women was that of prophet. There are many references to women prophesying in both Paul (1 Cor 11:5) and Luke (chp 2), but Acts 21:9 speaks very clearly of **the four daughters of Philip**, who prophesied in the Christian community of Caesarea. To prophesy did not mean to foretell the future, but to interpret the meaning of God's word for the congregation.

Teacher: Among the more famous missionary co-workers of Paul and renowned for their teaching of the faith was the couple **Priscilla** (also called Prisca) and Aquila. They were commended by Paul, in as much as they risked their lives for him, and were the ones who guided the learned Apollos to a more accurate understanding of the faith (Acts 18:26). No doubt in 1 Tim 2:12, women are forbidden to teach, but biblical scholars today consider this particular passage as 'polemical' and referring to a very specific and particular situation and not intended for the Church as a whole.[72]

Deacon: In Romans 16:1-2, we find **Phoebe**, a deacon, referred to as an "authoritative leader" or "protectress" of the community of Cenchrea, but women deacons are mentioned also in 1 Tim 3:11 and in several of the tomb inscriptions of the early centuries. Names like Maria, Timothea, Paula, Eugenia, appeared on epitaphs with the title 'deaconess' inscribed at the side.[73] The work of the women deacons was probably the same as that of the male deacons except perhaps that they worked only with women and children.

Founders and leaders of household churches and missionary co-worker: The church in Laodicea met in the home of **Nympha** (Col 4:15), who must have been a woman of some means; similarly, another community met in the home of John Mark's **mother** (Acts 12:12). So also **Priscilla** and her husband Aquila started churches in their home (1 Cor 16:19); another household church met in the home of Apphia and Archippus (Phil 2); **Lydia** was a businesswoman, who extended hospitality to Paul (Acts 16:15). Similarly, Mary, Tryphena, Tryphosa and Persis were some of those commended by Paul for their hard work.

Ministry of Widows: Finally, a special office in the early Christian community was the ministry of widows. These were not widows who needed community support, but were specially enrolled in the church to pray for the community (1 Tim 5:9-12). In the *Traditio Apostolica*, an early historical document, they are listed after the bishops, presbyters, deacons and confessors.[74]

If women were so active in the early church, one question that comes to mind is, 'Why don't we hear more about this in the New Testament? Why is there a silence in the reporting of their activities?' To this important query, two responses are given:

1) The common opinion: holds that the invisibility of women and the reason for the prohibitions and restrictions against women was because of the patriarchal nature of Roman culture and correspondingly of the Christian household churches.

2) The opinion of Adolf Harnack: According to this historian, some of the Christian churches, in opposing Montanism, (a sect which gave great prominence to women), were obliged to play down the role of women.[75]

Whatever be the reasons for the later demise of women's position of importance, one thing that stands out very clearly is that the Pauline churches showed a greater sense of equality between men and women. Women played very active and dynamic roles in early Christianity and perhaps that was one of the reasons for the tremendous growth of the community in the early ages. Similarly, today if we want renewal in the Church, if we want a Church that is alive, vibrant and vigorous, we need once again to have women assume positions of prominence and power.

34
What is Women-Church?

A woman in Mumbai, whose husband was an alcoholic and a wife batterer, was at her wits end. She had been to the doctor, to the counsellor, to the social worker, to the alcoholics anonymous, and to the local *Shiv Sena Shakha Pramukh*,[76] but nothing seemed to work. Finally, in desperation, someone suggested that she go to the local Mahila Mandal in her neighbourhood. She went to a meeting and shared her problem. The members of the Mahila Mandal discussed the problem with her and then decided to pay a visit to her husband. They went in a group, 'gheraoed' the husband and spoke sternly to him. The next day however the husband continued his routine of drinking and battering.

"Did anything change therefore? Or did the situation only get worse?" When the woman concerned was asked these questions, her answer was immediate and forthcoming: "Of course, the situation has definitely changed! The Mahila Mandal helped me to critically assess and handle my problem. Earlier I used to blame myself for my husband's behaviour. Now, I have a different perspective. The Mahila Mandal members enabled me to discuss, verbalize and talk over the matter. Now, I have the strength to face my husband. Even if he does not change, *my life will!*"

This incident, which took place in the nineties, reveals the role and purpose of the Mahila Mandals, women's groups in India, which have been in existence now for several decades. The women's movement in India has seen three phases: the first phase, associated with the Reform Movement in Modern India, protested against sati and the lack of women's education. The second phase originated with women's participation in the Independence movement and their involvement in land and peasant struggles. The third phase took off from the rape and anti-violence movement in the late seventies and early eighties. From the seventies and in the last phase especially, Mahila Mandal groups were the backbone of the women's movement. Recently however their role in consciousness raising has taken on momentous proportions and they have become a powerful agent of transformation in Indian society.

In the Catholic Church in the West, a similar movement has arisen that calls itself **Women-Church**. What does Women-Church mean? Are these groups of women who want to detach themselves from the Church because it is male-oriented? Or are these groups of women that want a separate Church of their own with their own priests? Or are these groups of women that desire an exodus from the Church because it does not permit equality for them?

Not at all!! None of these answers are true!! Women-Church refers to a group of women who really love the Church but want it to be purified of its human errors. They do not want to leave the Church. Instead, they want very much to stay within it and critique it from the inside. They feel that so long as the 'patriarchal under-standing' prevails within the Church, there is need and scope for women to critically assess it. In order to do that women need to have a space of their own, need to come together and articulate their own experience and communicate it with each other.[77]

Members of the Women-Church use the term 'defecting in place'. Defecting in place is a metaphor, which means both to stay and to leave. It means leaving the old way of relating and thinking, and being present in a whole new way.[78] Thus Women-Church consists of small groups of women who are taking charge of their spiritual lives in their own settings. They experiment with their own prayer services, para-liturgical ceremonies and alternative liturgies. Much like the members of the Charismatic Renewal, who, though loyal to the hierarchy are creating a new culture within the Church, Women-Church members are active participants of their local diocesan Church, but at the same time are generating a culture for a 'Church to emerge at the margins.'

From the time of Moses, the 'Church' has been an exodus community against structures of oppression. Women-Church too wants to be an exodus community against patriarchy. Women have to withdraw from male-dominated spaces so that they can gather and define their own experiences. They need separate spaces to develop this critical culture and both Mahila Mandals in Indian society and Women-Church members in Christianity are trying to achieve an autonomous ground from which to critique patriarchy. An analogy from history may make things clearer. The Chipko movement, spearheaded by women, brought an ecological consciousness, not only to central India but to other parts as well; so also, Women-Church members hope to bring about a greater consciousness of mutuality and equality within the entire Catholic Church.

Endnotes
ᘓ

1. Schussler Fiorenza Elizabeth, *In Memory of Her*. New York: Crossroads, 1983, p. 16
2. Haskins Susan, *Mary Magdalene: Myth and Metaphor*. New York: Riverhead books, 1993
3. Hamington Maurice, *Hail Mary?* New York and London: Routledge, 1995, p. 149
4. Hamington, ibid. ch. 6. "The Recasting of Marian imagery" p. 164ff
5. *Provisional Population Totals*. Census of India 2001, Paper 1 of 2001.
6. Liefeld Walter, "Women submission and Ministry in 1 Corinthians" in Mickelsen Alvera, Ed. *Women, Authority and the Bible*. Downer's Grove, Il. Intervarsity Press, 1986, p. 146. see also Schussler Fiorenza, *In Memory of Her*. op. cit. pp. 229-230
7. Conzelmann H., "1 Corinthians" and cited in Evans Mary, *Women in the Bible*. NSW, Australia: The Pater Noster Press, 1983, p. 95
8. Ringe Sharon, "A Gentile Woman's Story" in Russell Letty, ed. *Feminist Interpretations of the Bible*. Philadelphia: The Westminister Press, 1985, p. 71
9. Fitzmyer Joseph, *The Gospel according to Luke X–XXIV*. New York: Doubleday, 1983, p. 893
10. Schussler Fiorenza Elizabeth, *In Memory of Her*. op. cit. p. 165
11. La Verdiere Eugene, *Luke*. Metro Manila: St. Paul Publications, p. 153
12. Laland Erling, "Die Martha-Maria-Perikope in Lukas 10, 38-42" in *Studia Theologica*. 13 [1959] p. 70-85 and cited in Schussler Fiorenza Elizabeth, *In Memory of Her*. op. cit. p. 165 and p. 200
13. cited in Reid Barbara, *Choosing the Better Part? Women in the gospel of Luke*. Collegeville, Minnesota: The Liturgical Press, 1996, p. 149
14. Knutsen Galen, "The Feast of Mary Magdalene" in *Worship*. Vol 71, Number 3, May 1977, pp. 205, 212

15. Knutsen Galen, ibid. p. 206

16. Fox, Ruth, "Women in the Bible and the Lectionary" in *Liturgy.* 90 (May/June 1996) pp. 4-9, 15

17. Agnes Flavia, "Protecting Women against Violence?" in *Economic and Political Weekly.* Mumbai, April 25, 1992 p. WS-20

18. Crime in India, 1993 (National Crime Records Bureau, New Delhi) pp. 256-262

19. Griffin Susan, *Rape, the Politics of Consciousness.* San Francisco: Harper and Row, 1986

20. Howe Florence, "Sexual Stereotypes start early" in Ed. Rose, Peter ed. New York: St Martin's Press, 1979, p. 53

21. Mananzan Mary John, "Education to Femininity or Education to Feminism" in *Concilium.* 1991/6 London: SCM Press, p. 29

22. Mananzan, Mary John, ibid. p. 29

23. Jeanne Devos, Bharati Pflug, "The Houseworkers' Movement" in *Integral Liberation.* December 1997, Vol 1, No. 4, pp. 242, 243. See also: Pereira, Olinda *Domestic Workers Struggle for Life* (Summary of the All India Survey sponsored by the CBCI Commission for Justice and Peace) New Delhi: CBCI Commission, 1984

24. Cunningham Armacost Nicole, "Domestic Workers in India: A Case for Legislative Action" in *Journal of the Indian Law Institute.* Vol 36 No. 1, Jan-March 1994

25. Lardner Carmody, Denise, *Biblical Women, Contemporary Reflections on Scriptural Texts.* New York: Crossroads, 1988, p. 34

26. Srinivasan, S., "Taking domestic violence outside the walls of the home" Presentation to American Medical Women's Association, San Francisco, Nov. 13, 1999

27. For similar such charts see, Schaef Ann Wilson, *Women's Reality.* Minneapolis: Winston Press, 1981. Also, Carr Anne, "On Feminist Spirituality: in Ed. Conn Joann Wolski, *Women's Spirituality.* Mahwah, New Jersey: Paulist Press, 1986

28. Easlea Brian, *Fathering the Unthinkable: Masculinity, Science and the Nuclear Arms Race.* London: Pluto Press, 1983

29. Fergusson David, *The Cosmos and the Creator.* London: SPCK, 1998, p. 9

30. Brown Raymond, *Responses to 101 Questions in the Bible.* Mahwah, NJ: Paulist Press, 1990, p. 36

31. Hamington, Maurice, *Hail Mary?* New York and London: Routledge, 1995, p. 130ff

32. Hamington Maurice, *Hail Mary?* Ibid. p. 139ff

33. Roy May, *La Tierra en tiempo de globalizacion.* PASOS, 76, 1998, pp. 22, 24 translated by John Kater, Jr.

34. Ritzer George, *The McDonaldization of Society.* New Century Edition, Thousand Oaks, California: Pine Forge Press, 2000.

35. Ceresko Anthony, "Ecology and Genesis 1:26-28: An Interpretative Strategy" in *Ecological Concerns.* Ed. Joe Mattam, and Jacob Kavunkal, Bangalore: NBCLC, 1998, pp. 29-31

36. Ricoeur Paul, *The Symbolism of Evil,* Boston, 1969, p. 12ff

37. Chittister Joan, *Heart of Flesh.* Michigan, Novalis, Ottawa: William B. Erdmans Pub. Grand Rapids, 1998

38. Berger Peter and Luckmann Thomas, *The Social Construction of Reality.* New York: Penguin Books, 1967, pp. 106-109

39. Sen Ilina, "Fundamentalist Politics and Women in India" in *Mixed Blessings: Gender and Religious Fundamentalism Cross-culturally.* Ed. Brink Judy, Mencher Joan, London: Routledge, 1997, pp. 207-221

40. Hardacre Helen, "The Impact of Fundamentalism on Women, the Family and Interpersonal Relations" in *Fundamentalism and Society.* Eds. Martin Marty and Appleby R.S., Chicago: Chicago University Press, 1993 pp. 129-150

41. Schussler Fiorenza Elizabeth, *In Memory of Her.* op. cit. p. 208

42. Plaskow Judith, *Sex, Sin and Grace: Women's Experience and the Theologies of Reinhold Niebuhr and Paul Tillich.* Washington: University Press of Arizona, DC. 1980, p. 172

43. Proctor-Smith Marjorie, "Images of Women in the Lectionary" in *Concilium* December 1985 Ed. Schussler Fiorenza Elizabeth, and Collins Mary, Edinburgh: T & T Clark Ltd, p. 56

44. Weaver Mary Jo, *Springs of Water in a Dry Land: Spiritual Survival for Catholic Women Today.* Boston: Beacon Press, 1993

45. Fernandes Arcbhishop Angelo, "Fresh Hope for WWW—World Without War" in *Examiner,* Bombay, Jan 2000

46. Johnson, Elizabeth, *She Who Is.* New York: Crossroads, 1993 pp. 47-57

47. Jung Carl, *Collected Works, Vol IX.: The Archetypes and the Collective Unconscious.* Translated by Hull R.F.C., London: Routledge and Kegan Paul, 1968, second edition, p. 54ff.

48. Chakravarti Uma, *Economic and Political Weekly, April 29, 2000*

49. Ibid.

50. Whalen Michael, "In the Company of Women? The Politics of Memory in the Liturgical Commemoration of Saints—Male and Female" in *Worship.* Vol 73, Number 6, 1999, pp. 482-505

51. *India 1998.* Ministry of Information and Broadcasting, Government of India, New Delhi, 1998, p. 15

52. Healey Shevy, "Growing to be an Older Woman" in *Women and Ageing.* Ed. Alexander Jo et al., Calyx Books, Corvallis, Oregon, 1986 pp. 58-62. See also "Beyond Hags and Old Maids" in "*Women and Ageing*" ibid. pp. 63-67

53. Phipps William, *Assertive Biblical Women.* Westport, Connecticut: Greenwood Press, 1992, p. 83

54. *Lawyer's Collective,* June 1996, Vol 11, No. 6

55. Johnson Elizabeth, *Friends of God and Prophets.* New York: Continuum, 1998 pp. 151-153

56. D'Souza Betty, "A burning nightmare" in *Health and Nutrition.* Feb. 2001

57. Agnes Flavia, and Gowda Veena, *Church, State and Women.* Majlis, Santacruz, Mumbai, 2000, p. 39ff

58. Joint Statement by CBCI, NCCI and JWP. World Wide Faith News, Sunday Sept. 2, 2001

59. *Indian Express,* Sept. 7, 1997

60. cited in MacNicol Nicol, *Pandita Ramabhai.* Calcutta: Association Press, p. 63

61. Tilak D. N., *Pandita Ramabhai.* Maharashtrachi Tejasvini Pandita Ramabhai, Nashik, 1960, pp. 120-124

62. MacNicol, Nicol. *Ibid.* p. 140

63. Cited in Staffner Hans, *The Significance of Jesus Christ in Asia.* Anand: Gujarat Sahitya Prakash, 1985, p. 168

64. Aung San Suu Kyi, *Freedom from Fear: and other writings.* New York: Penguin Books, 1995

65. Schultz William, "Uncovering the Truth" in *America.* Nov. 13, 1999

66. Vawter Bruce, "Introduction to Prophetic Literature" in *New Jerome Biblical Commentary*, Eds. Brown Raymond, Fitzmeyer Joseph, Murphy Roland, Theological Publications in India, 1992, p. 187ff

67. *Bombay Times*. November 4, 2000

68. Sanjay Sangvai, *The River and Life*. Mumbai: Earthcare books, 2000. The Hindi words, *Jal Samarpan*. actually mean 'sacrificial death by drowning' and the slogan used is *'Dubhenge par nahin hatenge' [we will drown but we will not be moved]*

69. D'Mello John, "Paradigms for Feminization of the Church" in *Vidyajyoti Journal of Theological Reflection*. New Delhi, Feb 1999 p. 119ff

70. Brooten Bernadette, "Junia. . . outstanding among the Apostles" in Leonard Swidler and Arlene Swidler, eds. *Women Priests: A Catholic Commentary on the Vatican Declaration*. New York: Paulist, 1977, pp. 141-144

71. Schussler Fiorenza Elizabeth, "The Apostleship of Women in early Christianity" in Swidler Leonard and Swidler Arlene, eds. op. cit. pp. 135-140

72. Eisen Ute, *Women Office Holders in early Christianity*. Collegeville, Minnesota: The Liturgical Press, 2000, p. 101

73. Ibid., pp. 160ff

74. Ibid., p. 144

75. Harnack Adolf, *The Expansion of Christianity in the first three centuries*. Vol 2. Translated and edited by Moffat James, New York: G. P. Putnam's sons, 1904-5.

76. Shiv Sena, a political party in India. Shaka Pramukh is the leader of a geographical unit of this party.

77. Ruether Rosemary Radford, *Women-Church: Theology and Practice of Feminist Liturgical Communities*. San Francisco: Harper and Row, 1985

78. Winter Miriam Therese, *Defecting in Place: Women claiming responsibility for their won spiritual lives*. New York: Crossroads, 1994

Glossary Of Indian Terms

Arya Mahila Samaj—Organization for the Reform of Women

Adivasi—indigenous population (original inhabitants of the land)

Babri Masjid—Mosque built by the Moghul Ruler Babar

Bajrang Dal—aggressive political wing of the Bharatiya Janata Party

Chitpavan—the name of a special 'caste'

Dalit—Oppressed Group

Dharna—A unique form of protest by which the protester refuses to budge until some action is taken

Gherao—to surround in such a way as to prevent movement of the surrounded person. It has become an accepted form of protest in India.

Gram Sevikas—Village level social workers

Harijan—Untouchable

Jal Samarpan—sacrificial death by drowning. The slogan used is 'We shall drown, but we shall not be moved (*Dubhenge par nahi hatenge*).

Jawan—Soldier

Kar Sevak—Volunteer workers

Lok Sabha—Lower House of the Indian Parliament

Mahila Mandal—Women's group

Memsahib—Mistress of the House

Moksha—Salvation or Liberation

Narmada Bachao Andolan—Save the Narmada (River) Movement

Neythri—Women Leader

Padayatra—Protest march (literally, pilgrimage on foot)

Panchayat—Local Council

Pandita—Learned person or person well-versed in the Hindu Holy Books

Parsis—Followers of the Zoroastrian religion

Sangh Parivar—Group of organizations that equate Nationalism with Hinduism

Saraswati—Goddess of Learning

Saree —Indian woman's dress

Sepoy—Indian soldier in the time of the British Raj

Shastras—Hindu Holy Books

Vishwa Hindu Parishad—ideological wing of the Bharatiya Janata Party